THE RESOURCES OF MUSIC SERIES

Music drama in schools

THE RESOURCES OF MUSIC SERIES

General Editors WILFRID MELLERS, JOHN PAYNTER

Music drama in schools

EDITED BY
MALCOLM JOHN

CAMBRIDGE *at the University Press 1971*

Published by the Syndics of the Cambridge University Press
Bentley House, 200 Euston Road, London N.W.1
American Branch: 32 East 57th Street, New York, N.Y.10022

Library of Congress Catalogue Card Number: 70-145607

ISBN: 0 521 08003 7

Printed in Great Britain by
William Clowes & Sons Limited
London, Colchester and Beccles

Contents

Introduction

In seeking points of contact between drama and music in the field of secondary education there are several approaches available to the imaginative teacher. Opera is a highly sophisticated art form, which in its greatest moments embraces that concept one thinks of as total theatre. Works by Mozart, Verdi, Wagner and Britten demand a mature understanding beyond the reach of most school children. Our difficulty lies not in bringing children to opera or music drama but in realizing that such adult conceptions are for the most part irrelevant to their lives in today's urban, electronic, pop culture. Perhaps such art will become more meaningful to some children as they mature, but most will not appreciate its subtleties nor be impressed by its artifice and illusion until after they have left school. One needs to turn to other less technically demanding modes of expression which are more closely linked with their present needs and aspirations.

Singing and drama applied together to various aspects of school life and study is not new, and this has been practised in Great Britain and America for many years. History and geography offer scope for period and regional study of folk song, and English literature abounds with songs, ballads and verse, from pre-Shakespeare to post-Osborne. At the turn of the century Francis W. Parker created in his school in New England a situation where the emphasis was upon social learning through related projects utilizing techniques of dramatization. H. Caldwell Cook, teaching at the Perse school in Cambridge in 1915, insisted that the words for the songs in the children's plays be composed by the boys and that music could be borrowed from folk song collections. He suggested that it was better still if the children wrote their own music. Today many teachers of music encourage child composition in class, and most English teachers have come to realize the education value of child poetry. There appears to be considerable room for cross-fertilization within the school situation between music and English, and for a more effective use of time in the average curriculum whereby such stimulating co-operation might be allowed to occur.

In most primitive societies, many of whose patterns of life have been studied in detail, music cannot be separated from poetry and dance. It is in children's singing games and action songs as well as in their playground and street games that one finds the modern counterpart of this tribal activity. Teachers in infant schools maintain this 'whole' approach to the very young child's growth, and his necessary link with tradition. But more important is his need to express his primitive state through a combination of movement, singing and ritual. Singing games are usually children's adaptations of adult ballads arranged in verse and melody to which they walk, skip or side-step in the basic formations of the circle, the double line and the cross. Action songs appear to go one step further and are a means of teaching the child about his environment through organized play methods.

Many schools now insist upon 'movement' sessions for the young child. Ann Driver, a disciple of Emile Jacques Dalcroze, began the now well-established movement broadcasts by the BBC in 1930. The ideas of Mary Wigman, Rudolph Laban and Peter Slade have had a stimulating effect upon teachers who are concerned about the wholeness of body, mind and spirit. More and more we are coming to realize that one of the ills which besets modern education is the tendency to specialize at too early an age. Not only this, but one sees a distinct lack of efficient use of the young child's desire for, and need of, movement as an aid to the learning process. An encouraging sign in recent years is the realization that the work begun in the infant school with songs and games ought to be continued, developed and extended until the child is thirteen or fourteen years of age, thus carrying forward the essential 'play' activity which has been shown by studies of child behaviour to be very important. Recent writings of George Self, Murray Shafer, John Paynter, Gabriel Barnfield, Richard Courtney, Richard Addison and others stress in practical terms this unity of creativity, with particular reference to primary and early secondary school children. It would be interesting to note some of the past movements which have led up to this present one.

Friedrich Froebel's ideas about child education were formulated in Germany in the 1830s, and paved the way for a child-centred approach to learning. His play schools – kindergartens – placed considerable emphasis upon singing games. By the 1880s the training of teachers in England for the Froebel schools was exacting and demanding. Qualifying assistants had to be able to sing in tune and in time songs connected with the games, and to know keys, rhythm and pitch. The most interesting aspect of the syllabus at this early date was the conception of the unity of life, nature, art and occupation. However, even the idea of free play as advocated by Froebel had its difficulties. According to many teachers children lacked the imagination to play according to their own lights, and because of the educational value required of the songs certain 'improvements' had to be introduced by the adult. So it was insisted that a good kindergarten game should afford the opportunity for intellectual training, ethical teaching, physical exercise, dramatic action, musical and rhythmic training, and concise, simple and accurate language.

Here, then was an idealized concept of the educational function of the

singing game. The naturalness of Froebel's play schools came up against
opposition during the 1920s and 30s. This was not only the result of changes
wrought within the system but also the scientific approach of Dr Maria
Montessori, who paid several visits to England at that time. Froebel's 'Gifts'
were supplanted by Montessori's 'Materials' in many infant schools. The
child now played (worked) with specific materials in a prepared situation.
This play-education concept requires the use of quality sound sources in
school music and simple, strong platforms and stands in movement and
drama work. Power of invention is stimulated by efficient use of good materials. For instance, a 20-inch cymbal of high quality metal will yield more
varied results than ten cheap instruments of poor quality. Likewise, firm,
symmetrical rostra will be of more use in drama class than splintered,
wobbly ones.

At the time Montessori was visiting England two German artists were
experimenting with drama from different starting points. Carl Orff and
Berthold Brecht both continue to have a profound effect upon our present-
day approach to music drama involving young people. One quality which
they shared was that of simplicity. However, they also felt that society was at
a low ebb and were prepared to criticize it through their mature dramatic
works. As far as their work for children was concerned this – as with most of
their other work – was designed to entertain and instruct. Orff's main concern has been with the expressive and ritualistic implications of the elements of music and the theatre. In music these elements are rhythm and
melody; in the theatre they are gesture and group movement. Musical
harmony is a relative newcomer to western culture, and where Orff uses com-
binations of sounds in his stage works they are peculiarly elementary. Although a student of medieval German, Greek and Latin, and a practical man
of the theatre, Orff decided in 1928–9 to experiment with teachers in
Munich in an attempt to come to grips with the basic qualities of both music
and drama. Working through body movement, gesture, simple rhythms and
pentatonic (five note) melodies he succeeded in creating an ordered 'growth
in awareness' of language, music and simple body movement. Some years
later his findings were broadcast and published in Germany and eventually
translated into English. These findings formed the basis of his now well-
known five volumes of *Music for Children* [*Schülwerk*].

Why does a man organize a system of musical instruction when his main
interests are languages and the theatre ? The answer is surely that his concept
of a child's education is far wider and deeper than isolated subject matter.
Music, movement, language and design spill over into each other's domain
and not only does the child benefit but each aspect of creative art benefits
from the process. Orff's attachment to Greek and primitive cultures, the

world of myth and legend, of fairy tale and old traditions suits him admirably as an educationist forming the link between the intellectually sophisticated adult world of art and artifice and the children's world of play and pretence.

Thus a further link was formed between language, music and movement. The percussion instruments associated with Orff's name have been accepted with enthusiasm – and where expense forbids purchase, have been made – and his theories regarding the use of the pentatonic scale as a starting point as well as his inclusion of simple techniques such as ostinato, canon, and imitation have been absorbed by many teachers. However, the complete course is taught by a minority of enthusiasts, these usually being teachers who have attended courses and so gained an inside working knowledge of the variety of musical and language experiences available. What has happened is that *Music for Children* has sparked off a re-assessment of the function of music in schools throughout the world. In some cases the tendency has been to throw the creative responsibility entirely upon the child – in the Froebel–John Dewey tradition – in order to avoid imposing any preconceived adult rigidity of style. With encouragement and love, and under careful guidance in the right environment, the results are exciting. Yet in other cases the results seem to lack form and direction. It would appear that the great handicap to the successful use of *Music for Children* lies in the lack of teachers trained to think creatively, and who could adapt to aspects of the course in the limited time allotted to music and drama in most schools. At present this area of a child's development is stunted through undernourishment and the full potential of Orff's work is seldom realized.

Bertold Brecht has exerted a considerable influence upon major English playwrights, particularly since 1956 when John Osborne's *Look Back in Anger* was first produced. At least three of his plays are often performed in British schools – *Galileo*, *Mother Courage* and *The Caucasian Chalk Circle*. Through trial and error, and by means of a highly original approach to other writers' plays, Brecht developed an epic social drama. Often satirical, nearly always objective in its action and dialogue, it attempted to make people think rather than to involve them in an emotional or ritualistic way. His relevance to this symposium lies in his sharp social conscience, his poetically direct means of making his point and his integral use of music. These three aspects of his style are pertinent to most fifteen- to eighteen-year-old children living in a relatively rootless society where the purveyors of commercial 'pop', sensational headlines and stereotyped characters in comics and magazines find a ready market for their goods. This age group is attracted towards direct social comment in dramatic form, and towards the pseudo-ballad sung over a simple accompaniment. Writers like John Arden, Arnold Wesker and others have been influenced by Brecht's austere, no-nonsense approach to the theatre. Ballads (old and new), couplets, snippets of song and whole soliloquies sung to music find a place in our social drama of the 70s.

Brecht was not a trained musician, but more than any other writer of this era he had musical ideas in the back of his mind, and his plays are full of musical implications. Of forty plays published some thirty of them use songs, and nearly all of them contain incidental music. Three were written as scripts for operas – *The Threepenny Opera*, *Mahogonny* and *Lucullus*. Five complete plays were written for school children; two of these works were operas – *The Stable Boy* and *The One Who Says Yes*. The alternative ending to the latter work was suggested by the boys acting the parts, both decisions being matters for the mind rather than the emotions. The pseudo-ballad style of the songs included in the plays is irregular, colloquial and directly associated with the action. The intensity of the words breeds an intensity and simplicity in the tunes and accompanying instrumentation. Composers of stature collaborated with Brecht throughout his life – Hindemith, Weill, Dessau and Eisler – and to perform the verses unsung would be to miss the point of the drama. This comment could just as easily be applied to the songs from Shakespeare, of course. Brecht himself insisted that the playwright could work out his experiments in uninterrupted collaboration with actor and stage designer; he could influence and be influenced. The painter and the composer regained their independence, and could express their views of the overall theme by their own artistic means. The integrated work of art finally appears before the spectator as a bundle of separate elements.

Such an approach seems feasible for fifth and sixth form children. Those who have been encouraged to express themselves in creative writing and music ought to be encouraged to write their own social dramas, distilled from their observation and experience of life. Reference to Brecht's theatrical means, and to important contemporary dramatist's work would help to make such an enterprise workable and entertaining. From our point of view, the satisfaction – and inspiration – of his work lies not in the form itself, but in his command of form which can shape it to fit a content that matters. The means are often simple and familiar; the subtlety exists in their choice and combination.

Brecht, as well as Orff, points the way to combined dramatic expression, with the component arts maintaining much of their own separate qualities, even at the time of performance. And yet for Brecht the text remained uppermost. Above all, he had a social message to put across. With Orff the music has a slight edge on the other aspects of his drama. A perfect balance between forces involved would probably be impossible, for the person

xi

Introduction

responsible for the conception of a work for dramatic presentation must have a bias in one direction or the other. But these two men have provided a means of linking words, which tend to be the private domain of the language teacher, the singing and playing of instruments, which so often never escape from the grasp of the music teacher, and design and movement, both of which seldom venture beyond the precincts of the art room or the gymnasium.

There have been many fine stage works written for young players during the last forty years. Three of the most outstanding compositions are by Benjamin Britten. Other composers whose balance of music and drama has resulted in excellent works are Alan Bush, Hugo Cole, Malcolm Williamson, Richard Rodney Bennett and there are others. There is an increasing tendency for schools to perform musicals containing easier, more light-hearted songs and choruses, but which often lack the dramatic qualities of other more integrated works. *West Side Story*, *Oliver* and *Salad Days* have often been performed by schools, the first work being particularly difficult to produce. The final choice must be made in the light of the children's needs, age, capabilities and relative maturity, quite apart from the dramatic quality of the play concerned. The fact that the choice of play has been left to the teacher/producer has inspired many teachers to create their own work for a specific group of children whom they know very well.

Five contributions to this book are concerned with just such an approach, two are concerned with the pupils' own creative efforts, and the last shows how professional actors work in close co-operation with teachers and pupils in the familiar surroundings of classroom and hall. It is to be hoped that the enthusiasm of the contributors will stimulate other teachers to direct action and further experiment.

M.J.

A *preparatory school approach*

PAUL DRAYTON and HUMPHREY CARPENTER

The tendency of adults to separate music from play and drama is naturally reflected in the habits of their children (whether the adult be parent or teacher). Music is listened to passively on the radio, on recordings, and even at concerts, and at best is participated in by the playing of an instrument, while drama consists of the pantomime at Christmas and, if the teacher feels so inclined, the occasional classroom play.

Humphrey Carpenter adapts a modern 'classic' written by a distinguished adult in terms which appeal to the truly 'child-like' in all of us. Paul Drayton illuminates for us the razor's edge upon which a composer, dealing with words in a dramatic series of events, is constantly treading. The desire to create a rich experience for eleven- to thirteen-year-old boys becomes at times a matter of avoiding the weaknesses of existing forms such as eighteenth-century opera – where the main function of the music was to 'fill in' (in the form of the aria) – and the twentieth-century musical – where the music often serves as a vehicle to support lavish costumes and intricate stage-machinery. A successful attempt has been made to come to grips with the reasons for using music in an adaptation of a narrative and the means of doing this for young children.

Paul Drayton read music at Oxford, and is director of music at New College School, Oxford.

Humphrey Carpenter read English at Oxford, and produced *The Hobbit* at New College School while he was reading for a Diploma in Education. He is now a radio producer with the BBC.

'THE HOBBIT' (P.D.)
The idea of writing a stage version of J. R. R. Tolkien's book was strongly supported by its popularity and wide appeal among children and adults. Its exceptional quality, providing an enchanting blend of adventure, excitement, goodness and evil in conflict, and the inimitable Tolkien spirit of 'faerie', all set in a delightful atmosphere of remoteness and antiquity offered an irresistible challenge. Although somewhat in awe of the very completeness of the book – 'a world of its own' the reviews had said – I had never felt more sympathetic to the setting of words to music or more stimulated at the prospect of trying to capture some of their magic and

1

poetry in a score. It was with a feeling of slight ambivalence – a mixture of reverence and growing conviction – that I allowed the first musical ideas to take shape in my mind.

Work started after we received the author's permission to 'adapt' the story. After some preliminary sketches for songs, drawn up in piano score from March to June 1967, the dramatic adaptation was begun by Humphrey Carpenter about five months before the production, and in accordance with our usual practice (we had worked together before), the first sections to be dealt with were the ones which incorporated songs. One of my first thoughts was to attempt a synthesis of any groups of songs that might combine to make a larger musical complex of several units, since I feel it is essential to move from dialogue to music and vice versa as few times as possible, or the work will fall somewhere between the genres of drama and grand opera while possessing the unity and depth of neither. Having written a musical together before, we have already faced the problem of alternating between the two levels of communication involved – words and music – and I believe that few musicals have come near to solving the problem, if indeed they were trying. In practice it may seem of little consequence in the musical comedy if the occasional song intrudes into the play's progress, since the leisurely pace of the story is an intrinsic feature of the genre; but if the musical is to be more than entertainment on a relatively superficial level, one must first recognize its unsatisfactory nature as a unified form. It is hybrid by tacit definition.

In spite of all the arguments for the validity of 'stylized art-forms' – comic opera included – the fact remains that when dealing with the juxtaposition of music and dialogue characters in drama should not need to sing at all, and, if they are made to do so, the quality and depth of the music will alone be a justification of its presence. But even if it has a *per se* justification, it may cause a serious lapse of credibility when characters speak *and* sing in otherwise convincing situations. It is on this point that we set out with a distinct advantage; most characters in musicals and *opéras-comiques* would not sing when faced with similar situations outside of their musical environment, but Tolkien's hobbits, dwarfs, and elves often do sing. It is part of their nature to do so. As the story is in every other way true to its own laws, it seemed that music would be a completion of this self-sufficient and circum-scribed world rather than a doubtful addition to it.

It was now clear that the sort of music to be written should attempt to provide unobtrusive, authentic settings of the verses and to create an atmos-phere only where one would otherwise be left with a purely visual portrayal of the narrative. The balance of the drama should not be upset by the music but complemented by it in a restrained manner. *The Hobbit*'s non-human quality pre-supposes music that affords discreet yet almost continual enhancement of its moods rather than a sudden attempt to redefine them in another medium. This could best be achieved by making music the norm rather than the exception, with considerable incidental music underneath the dialogue and during changes of scene. In this context the songs would seem more logical and a higher degree of integration would occur. The result of our efforts, therefore, was nearer to opera than to anything else, both in the

EXAMPLE 1

GANDALF: Tea? No, thank you. A little red wine, I think for me.
THORIN: And for me.
DWALIN: And hot mince pies with sugar and cream!
BOMBUR: And saddle of mutton with lots of spuds!
FILI: And cakes!
KILI: And ale!
BALIN: And coffee!
DWALIN: And tea!
BOMBUR: And bread!
FILI: And cheese!
KILI: And toast!
BALIN: And butter!
THORIN: What about eggs?

amount of music used – over an hour in a total of $2\frac{1}{4}$ hours of drama – and in the more elevated tone of the music itself. But whereas the basis of much operatic structure is the solo aria, and perhaps ensemble as well, in the case of the *Hobbit* score it is the chorus. It achieves the depersonalizing effect which aids in reflecting the timelessness of the book, and from a practical viewpoint it is unlikely that a small school could provide more than a couple of boys who could act and sing solos equally well.

A method of transition which we often referred to was that of moving from dialogue alone to dialogue over quiet music, to rhythmic speech over music, leading finally to singing. For example, in scene 2, in which the dwarfs visit Bilbo unexpectedly and make peremptory demands for food, consume it greedily and then wash up, this approach was used. The words were adapted so that each dwarf in turn might demand what he wanted to eat, moving in natural speech rhythm but fitting neatly over a recurring musical idea – pizzicato chords – and working to a climax, supported by an orchestral crescendo (see Example 1).

The musical idea which had been discreetly introduced in this way was then used as the basis for a complete song and expanded considerably (see Example 2).

We made it our policy to precede the actual singing of a song with a section of introductory dialogue over subdued introductory music, this usually being enough to mitigate the dialogue–music transition. There were similar arrangements in reverse – moving from music and singing back to dialogue – but this did not always seem so necessary. As mentioned earlier, we were helped enormously by the fact that singing is firmly implanted in the natures of the Tolkien genera, so that when Thorin says 'Now for some music', we are secure in the knowledge that he really means it, not because he feels it is time he gave a cue for music, but because he is a dwarf of Middle-Earth.

At the end of the school's summer term I looked in the book for sections that might be devoted entirely to music, over which voices might speak and sing by turn, and the most obvious section was at the very end of the story. In this there are three important songs separated by narrative and dialogue, and it seemed appropriate to link these into a finale of several musical units, incorporating all the material in the last chapter of the book. The first is a song of triumph sung by the elves on the death of the dragon, the second a lullaby sung by the elves to the weary Bilbo, and the third is sung by Bilbo himself; 'Roads go ever on'. This last song provides a key to the whole story, expressing the simple hobbit's wonder at the wideness and mystery of the world; after the turmoil of dragon-killing and battle it was vital to end in a purely reflective vein.

EXAMPLE 2

We decided to use the 'Roads' song as a unifying motif, a recurring theme representing the length of their journeying and the passing of time. It would be sung several times by the dwarfs on the road, and by the hobbit himself, in a wistful and subdued fashion, right at the end. The following layout emerged from the book's last chapter.

The narrator begins by saying that Bilbo and Gandalf had many hardships and adventures before they got back, but they eventually arrived again at the brink of the valley of Rivendell on May the first. During this narration and under the ensuing dialogue between Bilbo and Gandalf the introductory music begins, fragmentary at first – short phrases and rests – then leading into a full-blooded paean of victory sung by all the chorus. The first verse is

2

loud, with tremolando strings (see Example 3). The second verse ('The stars are far brighter') is taken very gently with string harmonics, harp and glockenspiel, and in the third verse ('O! Where are you going, so late in returning?') the same theme is taken faster and slightly extended, in a higher key. The music continues in the orchestra, treating the same motifs in fugato passages, while the narrator describes the scene as the elves gather around to hear Gandalf tell of their adventures. The music

EXAMPLE 3

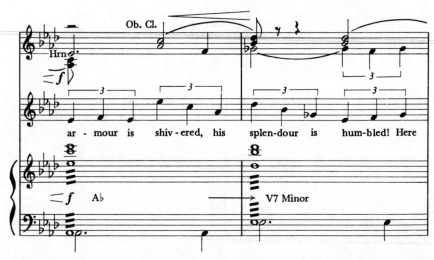

gradually subsides until it slips gently into a lullaby. The narration over, the elves sing once more ('Sing all ye joyful, now sing all together'). I did not limit the volume here in spite of its being a lullaby; Bilbo's subsequent remark, 'Your lullaby would waken a drunken Goblin' should carry full significance!

In the second verse of the lullaby a wordless descant is added (see Example 4). In the dreamy third verse the elves divide into three-part harmony, fading right away so that dialogue may follow naturally. As it does so, the musical material of the lullaby is gently developed in the orchestra with a 'running down' effect and a change to a lower key. The narrator tells of their departure from Rivendell – mimed on the stage – and they are on the road once more. Echoes and memories of their adventures recur with snatches of themes in the orchestra, until the now thoughtful hobbit begins to sing the final song. Gandalf delivers the clinching line: 'My dear Bilbo, something

EXAMPLE 4

is the matter with you. You are not the hobbit that you were!' Now the
entire company – offstage except for Bilbo and Gandalf – sing very softly a
second verse of the 'Roads' song, with muted strings, low woodwind, and an
unbroken chain of triplet figuration on the harp. These bars are the heart of
the score (see Example 5). The end of the piece and the end of the story comes
with a canonic reiteration of the first phrase of the 'Roads' song until the

EXAMPLE 5

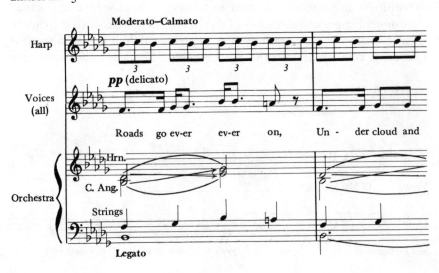

un - der star, yet feet that wan - der - ing have gone

sound is almost lost in the distance, and with the final orchestral cadence Bilbo has arrived home with the words 'Well, I'm back.'

This musical structure, spanning the final chapter of the book and lasting twelve minutes, embodies all the most significant motifs that were used in the score. At this point it would be useful to say a little more about the motifs themselves. Apart from the hobbit Bilbo and the wizard Gandalf there are four principal groups in this simplified version of the story; the dwarfs, the elves of Rivendell, the goblins and the men of Laketown.

The dwarfs are represented by the first phrase of their song 'Far over the Misty Mountains cold', which is the only other section of music comparable in length to the finale. It occurs in scene 2 and was intended to act as a counterbalance to the finale. The phrase which occurs with ever-increasing intensity and thereafter becomes associated with the dwarfs is shown in Example 6.

EXAMPLE 6

Slow (Voices)

The elves are announced by a simpler phrase, rather like a horn call (see Example 7). This derives from the chorus they sing when they first appear at

EXAMPLE 7

Rivendell, in scene 5, although it is darkly hinted at in the dwarf-song of scene 2 when the elves are mentioned. It pervades the whole score, particularly in the finale, either as a direct and sprightly contrast to the more brooding dwarf motif, or as a distant horn call, or just as an echo of the elf-magic hidden in the orchestral texture.

EXAMPLE 8

Gandalf was given his own short musical 'label', but to herald him with it in the most obvious places – appearing from nowhere to resolve a crisis – seemed so trite and reminiscent of the worst type of adventure film, that his theme occurred infrequently.

The goblins were denoted by a heavy, martial sequence of two recurring chords (see Example 8), but owing to their limited participation in the drama, this was of little structural significance.

The men of Laketown who first appear at the beginning of the second half (scene 10) have a robust chordal idea which introduces their song, 'The king beneath the mountain', and looms large in the second half of the score (see Example 9).

EXAMPLE 9

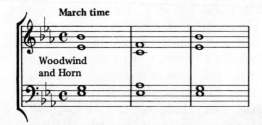

Bilbo's hobbit motif was a more rustic tune (see Example 10), appearing often, and sometimes in the most unlikely places.

EXAMPLE 10

Perhaps the most essential motif, from a purely functional point of view, was the one depicting the effect of the magic ring (which made the wearer invisible) (see Example 11). In this way, when Bilbo first discovers the ring and whenever he becomes invisible by wearing it, the ring motif is heard, sometimes isolated and sometimes (as in the song he sings at the spiders – see Example 12) incorporated suddenly in the middle of a passage of music

EXAMPLE II

(String Harmonics)

and sustained until he takes it off. And so the spiders' pursuit of Bilbo, who annoys them by disappearing and reappearing, is made clear to the audience, even though the boy involved never in fact perfected a technique of dematerializing! Gollum, who appears only once (scene 7), needed no motto-theme. His identity should be no more specific in the music than it is in the story. However, much thought was given to the setting of his riddles, and we found that the maximum amount of malevolence could be extracted by having them spoken in a slow measured rhythm, with sibilant relish over a sparse musical background – strings playing very quiet tremolandos near the bridge and flutter-tongued flutes. Gollum's riddles alternated with the hobbit's more homely ones, spoken over familiar musical material, and an eerie, cavernous feeling was given to the whole scene by a tape of dripping water, pre-recorded through a reverberation unit.

EXAMPLE 12

The method of 'motivic identification' I have outlined proved an invaluable aid in constructing a logical and unified score, and it is significant that I did not have to go out of my way to incorporate the various motto-themes for they usually slipped neatly into place, often combining with each other in a contrapuntal way. The whole exercise tended to confirm my belief that certain Romantic composers, working on a larger scale, were using the 'leitmotif' technique less as a purely dramatic means of identifying characters, emotions and ideas, than as a practical aid to composing a long yet coherent score.

In the battle scene (scene 13), the appropriate motifs were combined to represent the conflicting parties. Dwarfs, men, goblins and Gandalf were all accounted for in the music, and the sequence culminated with a unison, fortissimo statement of the hobbit theme as Bilbo was stunned by a blow from a goblin and the stage was darkened. The battle was dispensed with in about a minute, being mimed on stage with stylized movements – the goblins in slow motion attacking the long line of men and dwarfs from the rear – and the whole suffused by a demonic red glow.

The overriding considerations for the orchestration of the score were that the orchestra should not be so large that it might drown the boys' voices and that it should not require instrumentalists who were not locally available. I decided upon a dozen players, with the string quintet as the basic unit. Woodwind (with players doubling) were necessary for colour and 'body', as were also a wide range of percussion instruments. It turned out that the most convenient ensemble was as follows: flute doubling piccolo, oboe doubling cor anglais, clarinet doubling bass clarinet, bassoon, horn and harp; two percussion players with two timpani, side drum, bass drum, cymbals, suspended cymbal, glockenspiel, xylophone, wood-blocks, triangle and whip; two violins, viola, cello and double bass. At the risk of being a little ambitious, I considered that forces less than these might well be restricting in depicting the wide colour-range of the Tolkien palette.

One initial problem in the vocal scoring was deciding whether to enlist the services of parents and friends to provide altos, tenors and basses, but owing to lack of time and the complications of arranging parental rehearsals, we favoured treble voices. Since many boys were choristers they could easily be divided up into two or three parts when the need arose. Three-part dividing occurred most often when an offstage chorus (sung by the portion of the cast waiting in the wings) added a descant to an onstage vocal line, either one or the other being divided into two. Offstage singers can provide a risk of going sharp unless the accompaniment is sufficiently audible to them and they resist the urge to project their voices too much. The only place where this problem did arise was at the end of the finale – a lightly accompanied three-part canon sung offstage – and though the singers were aware of this tendency, it was a continual threat, guaranteed to keep everyone on their toes to the very end.

The 'narrator' technique provided the simplest method of keeping the story moving over long descriptive passages; weary motions of walking and climbing were mimed on stage as the narrator described, over music, particular stages of the journey. A simple tableau sometimes sufficed, with the delightful words being vivid enough to create the necessary atmosphere. These narrative passages over music did provide certain difficulty in their timing. In writing the music I tried to estimate the time the passage would take to speak. With practice, the boy concerned coped admirably, often reaching his final word one beat before the chorus were due to sing the next section.

Rehearsals began early in the Christmas term, giving twelve weeks in which to assemble the whole production. We could not have managed with less time owing to the length and comparative complexity of the play, and for much of this period there were rehearsals on every weekday. During the first half of the term there were two or three rehearsals a week which only involved the learning of songs. These were learnt from memory since the cost of duplicated vocal parts is prohibitive, both from the point of view of expense and because of the undue reliance which would have been placed on them by boys who find sight-reading music an easier task than memorizing it. During the second half of the term the two aspects of music and production began to be combined and were eventually inseparable in all rehearsals. After reaching the expected 'saturation point' and giving a week's rest to the singers, things began to slip into place more confidently.

A third and equally important feature of these rehearsals was the treatment of what might be called the choreographic sequences. Actual dance movements were not used, but certain scenes required movements to be measured carefully against the music. Once the actors knew where they should be at certain key points in the score, it was really a question of patient repetition until they sensed the amount of time available and the speed at which they should move. The most extensive sequence of this type was in scene 9, when the great spiders of Mirkwood crept up to the sleeping dwarfs and ensnared them in their webs. This was done in slow motion to create a dreamlike impression in which the struggles of the dwarfs would seem quite futile against the relentless advance of the spiders. The music provided a gradual build-up with a menacing, angular motif on the upper strings over a plodding ostinato in the harp, cello and bass, ending in a shrieking discord on the woodwind as Bilbo stabbed one of the spiders; the xylophone and pizzicato strings provided a spikey accompaniment to its death-throes.

There were four separate rehearsals for the orchestra – excluding dress rehearsals. It was made up of parents, local undergraduates, and senior pupils from near-by schools. At one stage I had considered including orchestral parts easy enough to be played by boys in the school. However, I abandoned the idea because it would have enlarged the size of my task out of all proportion, taking much more time to do credit to the story with strictly limited resources, and also because our best choristers tend to be our best instrumentalists and these would be required to sing. In the matter of hand-written orchestral parts we are convinced from experience that the standard of part-copying bears a direct relationship to the standard of orchestral playing, and although writing out the parts in Indian ink – with sufficient cues and page-turns in convenient places – can take up much time, in the end it always seems to have been worth the effort. Boys were encouraged to turn up at some of the orchestral rehearsals in order to familiarize themselves with the real sound of the music after singing so much to a piano.

By the time of the first performance, most members of the cast, singers of varying degrees of accomplishment, were in a sufficient state of mild nervousness to ensure their concentration, and ready to rise to the occasion in the peculiarly resilient way that young boys have, even after weeks of exhausting rehearsal. They also managed to sustain a high level of concentration throughout the performance ($2\frac{1}{4}$ hours, excluding the interval), through performances on four successive days. Although children of ten to thirteen years must clearly not be over-taxed, particularly if understudies are not available, I believe this shows that one can draw on enormous resources of stamina so long as the project confronting them can retain their enthusiasm and dedicated effort.

From the outset we were helped by the almost unanimous praise accorded to the book by children of a wide age-range (not to mention their parents), and to give the final performance before Professor Tolkien himself was an added excitement. Fortunately he seemed reasonably content with what he saw and heard!

On the technical side of production, it was in the last hectic weeks that many pressing tasks of a practical nature had to be dealt with on the stage, and we are indebted to our 'resident technical director' – the head of science and mathematics – who build the set I had designed, supervised lighting, sound-cues and effects. We agreed on the necessity of a wide rostrum for the upstage acting area, since the stage was too deep and high for an unraked auditorium. To this we added three arches spanning the front of the rostrum, with wide, curved steps passing up through the central arch. Jagged, stylized rock shapes were cut from hardboard to mask the front of the rostrum on each side of the steps and to break up the area between the rear of the rostrum and the back wall. These 'rocks' were painted an even grey–blue all over, and the steps a pale yellow. The arches, each made from three lengths of flexible, white curtain rail, spread out in three directions in the manner of vaulting so as to give a bare, skeletal effect that might be interpreted as the trees of Mirkwood or the pillars of the great hall of Laketown or simply as all-purpose decoration not really obtrusive enough to impose any concrete idea on the audience's imagination.

Thus we had a permanent setting for the whole story, to which projected images on the back wall added not only depth and colour, but also a definition of the actual place at any given time. Two overhead projectors sited just offstage were used to project half of a picture each (drawn with coloured felt pens on the transparent strip of film) on to the back wall, one on the right side, the other on the left. The oblique angle of projection made it necessary to draw in deliberately distorted perspective, very much on a trial and error basis. The boys who operated the projectors in the performance had to spend some time in practising the technique of winding the rolls at the same speed. The scenes had to match up! Near the end of the journey, the projections were wound back quickly through scenes 15–5. The flashing past of these previous scenes well suggested the passing of time and the many strange places on the journey, until, with convenient speed, they reached the valley of Rivendell, which forms the back-drop to the finale.

There were many time-consuming jobs to be done, from the sorting out of costumes and props, the design of the programme (with a map for the uninitiated), the angling of lighting and the painting of the set, to the recording of tapes for the most diverse and eccentric sound effects. These included: 'dragon snoring', 'dragon flies overhead, is shot and dies', 'approaching goblin army' and so on. In scene 12, when the dragon, Smaug, speaks spine-chillingly from offstage through an electric megaphone, his words were backed by a continual, disembodied organ-like sound; this was a specially monitored recording of chords played on a piano – yet another addition of our long tape of special effects.

When one is heavily involved in this way with the many individual facets needing urgent attention, it is a stringent test of the children's capacity to keep up to the mark in their own problems of script, movement and singing. When one finds boys rehearsing their own parts, prompted not by a master but by a healthy mixture of conscientiousness and apprehension at the coming event, it is a gratifying reminder of the value of such an enterprise in cultivating the discipline of a team effort based less on physical or academic criteria than on artistic initiative and sensibility.

How far would school productions of operas and plays ever progress if they were considered the exclusive reserve of music directors and English teachers? Not before *The Hobbit* or since has such a wide variety of assistance been necessary, and the assistance was forthcoming to a degree one hardly dares to expect from people so heavily preoccupied in their own spheres. Teamwork, in a preparatory school as anywhere else, is the life-force of such a project, but it is, of course, a means to an end. The end in this case was the enjoyment of those taking part. This was always the supreme consideration, and in this respect at least I know we were successful.

THE ADAPTATION AND PRODUCTION (H.C.)

In adapting the book to play form – fifteen scenes in all – I had two main principles in mind. First, to retain the style and character of the book, and second, to impose dramatic shape upon it. The first simply involved using the existing dialogue wherever possible, and consciously adopting Tolkien's style when continuations and alterations had to be made. The second principle was the harder of the two, involving greater thought and reflection. As it stood the book was too long for the stage. If performed uncut it would take more than three hours; so I cut out the incidents not absolutely vital to the plot – the trolls, the wolves, the eagles and Beorn. None of these occupy a strong place in the saga; they are trimmings, and easily disposed of.

However, I was still left with an unsatisfactory story for our purposes. The book becomes confused with the slaying of Smaug, the dragon. In the book this takes place away from the centre of the action, in Laketown, and the dragon is killed by a character introduced for the purpose, Bard the Bowman. To impose unity I introduced Bard in the first Laketown scene, making him the Master's steward, and brought him, with his men, to the mountain for the argument, so that Smaug could be killed in the centre of the action – the mountain – and by a character already important to the play. This is the only major alteration I made to the book.

Other alterations were of two kinds: making extended use of the songs, and making the play more relevant to the whole 'Ring Cycle'. The 'Roads' song, which is a recurring 'journey' motif in *Lord of the Rings* (a later book), served a similar purpose in the play, and I borrowed words from the other books as well as adding some of my own. The process of 'Tolkienizing' the play was most amusing; by reference to the other books I could embroider the genealogies and names of characters in the play, giving a more authentic ring than it actually possesses, having been written before *Lord of the Rings*. The final alteration was to extend the significance and importance of the ring in the play.

We worked on a tiny stage, about 18 feet wide and 15 feet deep, with no flying height at all; we had 3 feet of wing space. Having decided to use over-head projectors for the setting, we had to squeeze these up against the back wall and take 'keystone' distortion into account when making the drawings. The set was simple: the projection area masked by black drapes and outlined by a central arch halfway downstage, which was continued to left and right. Black drapes were also used as 'legs' to mask the wings. The central piece was a rostrum about 1 foot 6 inches high extending right across the back half of the stage. This was reached by a wide pair of steps centre stage which could accommodate three people on each tread. This width facilitated grouping for the 'Roads' and other sequences. The essence of the set was simplicity – black drapes and yellow front to the rostrum.

Costumes were a problem. The budget was of necessity small, and so was our wardrobe. Luckily we were helped by another school, which gave us the run of its extensive wardrobe. We were able to produce costumes that were adequate and colourful. No attempt was made at 'realistic' costuming or make-up. The dwarfs were distinguished by beards and blue tights, with different coloured tunics. The men wore black tights, chain-mail tunics. The elves wore black tights and silver tunics. The goblins were dressed completely in black with masks. Bilbo wore a smoking-jacket, plus-fours and a red bowtie. and the hairy feet were made by the judicious use of gym-shoes and an old fur cape. Gandalf was dressed in grey and silver. These basic distinctions between 'breeds' accentuated the divisions clearly enough. Make-up was kept to a bare minimum.

Lighting was another problem, not only because of lack of lamps, but also because of the small scale of the stage. We managed with six '23' pattern spotlights, two '123' pattern spotlights, two floodlights, a six-way batten, and a twelve-way groundrow for effects. The board had only eight dimmer channels, and by cross-switching and careful planning we were able to run all cues on the dimmers. The lighting plot was quite complicated as it included the fading in and out of the projectors, and there were more than fifty lighting cues. The board was operated by two boys under the supervision of the technical director.

Sound effects were used quite extensively. Apart from one or two local effects – china crash and bell – most were taped. Two naturalistic sounds were bird-song and a stream for Rivendell, but the greatest problem was the creation of the unique 'dragon' and 'goblin army' effects mentioned earlier. With imagination and professional equipment – in a local recording studio – and two or three boys to shout and scream, *very* satisfactory noises emerged.

A *middle school project*

IRIS DU PRÉ

A group of second form grammar-school boys and girls here reveal an ability to invent melodies and to set words to music – and do so within a dramatic framework. The songs become vehicles for extra-musical expression, and their mood ranges from repetitive work song to black magic incantation. The musical invention has involved movement and design from the very beginning. Although the advantages of working with a small group are obvious – a different approach would have been taken with a larger class – the final outcome of this long project was that many older boys and girls at the school took part in the performances.

Iris du Pré studied at the Royal Academy of Music and the Dalcroze School of Eurhythmics. She is a governor of the Central Tutorial School for Young Musicians and has taught at comprehensive and grammar schools.

'THE VIGIL'

I have always felt that, with encouragement, children could compose. From an early age they are able to express themselves freely in mime, painting, drawing, acting, dancing and inventing stories, but very little musical composition is attempted. It is in nursery and primary schools that musical composition should be an exciting activity; stories could be illustrated with percussive and melodic sounds improvised by the children. They should be encouraged to improvise tunes to rhymes, even to short sentences. In fact a short play could be turned into an improvised opera with the children singing their lines instead of saying them.

It is in the primary school that children ought to learn the rudiments of music. Most children arriving at grammar schools have never heard of crotchets, quavers, scales and time signatures. If the theory of music could be taught in a practical way to *young* children, some of them at least would find that they could themselves put down their own hummings and drummings on paper.

Over the years, I have taught music for the General Certificate of Education at ordinary and advanced levels at a comprehensive school and at a grammar school, and have been most concerned that the syllabi contain no imaginative or creative work. The harmony and counterpoint paper demands a knowledge of 'rules'. Children become inhibited by what they may or may not do. There is no room for experiment, imagination or discovery – no 'fresh air' – just stuffy text-book harmony.

So I decided to encourage a dozen or so children at Apsley Grammar School who had opted to do music instead of a second language in their second year, to write music before they had any knowledge of text-book harmony. I thought that an opera would be ideal for the children to compose because the atmosphere, moods and characters would be suggested by the libretto. I found a dramatic Russian story for which a member of the English staff wrote the libretto; as it was a gripping and sinister tale I felt that it would help the children to be more daring in their choice of melodies and harmonies.

The plot of *The Vigil* concerns Vassili, a Russian boy, who surprises the tsar's daughter in the act of removing her head in order to comb her hair. Thereafter the witch–princess pursues Vassili intending to destroy him, and finally demands that he shall watch alone all night by her coffin when she dies. In the highly dramatic last scene Vassili, advised by his school-teacher

EXAMPLE I

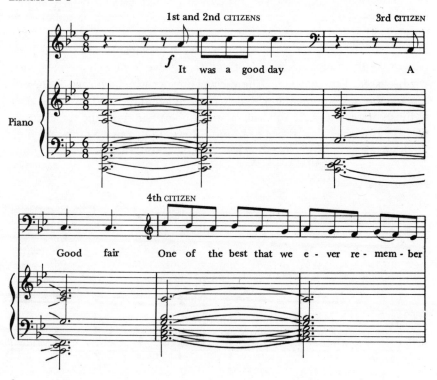

(another magician), sings psalms all night within a magic circle into which the princess and her demons try in vain to break. They are eventually banished by cock-crow, and the tsar, with his court, arrives and adopts the boy as his son and heir.

When the libretto of the first scene was ready and duplicated I gave a copy to each child in the special music lesson and instead of reading it through they sang it through. It was an hilarious lesson – the opera was under way and the opening phrases were written down immediately (see Example 1).

There was no difficulty in apportioning the work as most of the children knew which 'bits' of the scene they would like to compose. Sometimes two children worked together. I suggested that instead of using major or minor scales the melodies and harmonies should be composed from a scale having semitones between the second and third, and sixth and seventh degrees, as this would give the opera some sort of unity – there were thirteen composers at work – and help the children to avoid diatonic melodies and harmonies. Example 2, sung by the school-teacher, an old woman, uses this formation (the Dorian mode).

Of course we did not keep slavishly to this idea. The children learned how to use various compositional techniques: repetition, sequence, canon, ground bass, a musical figure as an accompaniment, and raising the pitch in more exciting and intense passages.

Some of the children's first attempts were unsingable and would have been difficult to memorize so I played them several of Schubert's songs; we discussed them and noted the various devices which he used. Someone remarked how a commentator's voice rises higher and higher from the start to finish of a horse race, and said how Schubert had done the same sort of thing in a musical way in *The Erl King*. This gradual raising of the melodic pitch was used to good effect when Vassili looks into the princess's window

EXAMPLE 2

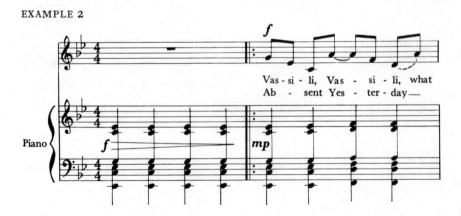

and observes her sitting in front of a mirror, lifting off her head. His voice rises as he sings what he sees, until eventually he breaks into *Sprechgesang* – an exciting, non-pitched recitative – still with his voice rising, until he ends with a shriek 'Am I mad ?' (See Example 3.)

EXAMPLE 3

Lost   in   her gol - den   hair   Twist -ing the gleam-ing

strands   And lift-ing her,   lift-ing her,   lift-ing her   head right

off   Putting it   on her lap

The first attempt at providing the chordal accompaniment to this recitative was very tame, but the composer soon realized that the chords must be as exciting as the melody and so experimented at the piano with discords.

Again, the children discovered from Schubert how often he used one musical figure throughout a song as an accompaniment to a melody – for example, *The Trout* – and they were surprised to find that the effect was not boring. In Example 4, sung by the princess's three waiting-women as they wait for the doctor's report on her as she lies mortally ill, the composer uses a simple musical figure throughout the aria. In this same aria there is good use of repetition of a musical phrase.

EXAMPLE 4

EXAMPLE 5

The children soon discovered the value of this device and how important it was that a musical idea should be heard more than once. They became aware of the usefulness of sequences, and throughout the opera tried to write in a practical way so that soloists and chorus would be able to learn their parts without undue difficulty. Canonic devices were used many times, and a ground bass in fifths gave the right atmosphere in 'Noses to the grind-stone' (see Example 5). This was sung by peasant workers returning from their holiday.

Some arias were composed during a class lesson. One child would sing a melody for the first line of a verse, and another would add the melody for the second line, and so on. This approach combined composition with aural training, for having sung a phrase the child wrote it on the blackboard, or told me what to write. I found this method a stimulating way of composing, there being much discussion as to the merit and suitability of each phrase. Melodies composed in this way formed the witch's psalm-like recitatives to which the children enjoyed writing dissonant chords as an accompaniment. Example 6 is sung by the princess–witch when she is dying – she says she will take Vassili to Hell with her.

EXAMPLE 6

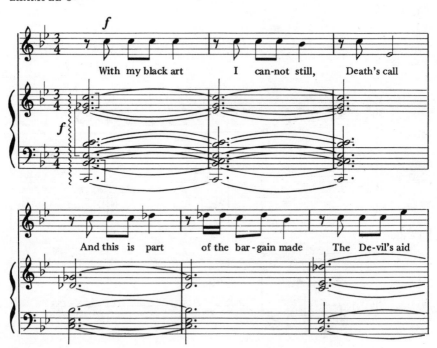

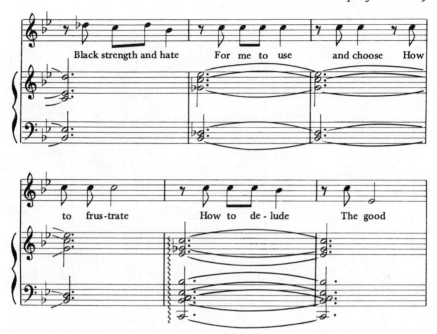

The final chorus in the last scene was also composed in class, as was the music for the doxology which was sung in three different versions in the last scene.

In choosing the accompanying instruments for the singers the probable 'weight and volume' of solo or chorus sound from the stage was kept in mind. From the first year at Apsley Grammar School each class has it own orchestra and rehearses once a week in one of the two weekly music lessons. Among the thirteen composers was a violinist, a double bassist, a trumpeter, a bassoonist, oboist, clarinettist and pianist. Except for the final choruses – which were scored for a Haydn-type orchestra – the arias and choruses were accompanied by one, two or three instruments with percussion, or by piano and percussion. The cello is used frequently throughout – perhaps because my daughter Jacqueline had promised to play in the school orchestra for one of the performances!

In the final scene, which takes place in a great cathedral, imaginative use is made of percussion and a tape-recording of Arctic wind. The witch rises from her coffin, emerges, and conjures up evil spirits to distract Vassili who at that moment is intoning psalms. The witch sings the doxology backwards on a staccato vocal figure which rises in pitch as she becomes angrier at being unable to distract Vassili from his psalm singing (see Example 7).

EXAMPLE 7

The children decided that it didn't matter if the witch's notes didn't 'fit' with Vassili's, in fact they had discovered the necessity of using dissonances to give a feeling of tension. When the witch returned to her coffin they relaxed into *normal* harmony for the doxology.

The opera took sixteen months to write after which the parts were professionally copied from the score and rehearsals began for the 130 children who were involved. Encouraging children to act and sing at the same time is not easy as from the age of twelve most children tend to be self-conscious when it comes to doing anything alone on the stage, whereas younger children usually act naturally and love pretending to be someone else.

For the composers it was a great day when we gave the first of three performances, and when they took their bow at the end of the final performance I am sure they felt that all these months of hard work had been worth while – especially after two national newspapers commented favourably on our efforts! Since the opera one of the composers has written a bassoon concerto which he performed with the school orchestra, and a special music group in their second year at school contributed two carols towards an 'Offering of Six Carols' which were sung at the annual carol concert. The remaining four carols were composed by older children.

A *secondary modern musical*

DAVID WILDMAN and HARRY W. JACKSON

The following description will be familiar to many readers in the United Kingdom:

'The school occupies two groups of buildings one mile apart by road, with specialist facilities about equally divided. This entails constant movement between buildings, which, with the two lunch sittings at each site, makes out-of-school activities dependent upon pupils staying late and missing school transport facilities. The school has a long sporting and athletic tradition as well as a more recent one in music and drama, and much co-operation is required to prevent the two interests clashing. General Certificate of Education 'O' level and Certificate of Secondary Education examinations are taken in the two fifth forms, and about fifteen pupils a year go on to various grammar schools. Soon the school is due to become a Middle School (9–13 years) under the reorganization scheme for comprehensive education in the area. The present grammar school will become the senior Comprehensive School.'

Against this typical background David Wildman and Harry Jackson outline the steps which led to the creation and production of *Vendetta*.

David Wildman trained at Leeds College of Art, and holds the National Diploma in Design and the Art Teacher's Certificate. He has worked in Bradford Civic Playhouse, Bingley Little Theatre and the Ilkley Playhouse, and has had exhibitions of theatre design. He is head of the art and drama department at Ilkley Secondary School.

Harry Jackson studied at Wymondham Training College and the Midland School of Music, and has taught all ages of children in Somerset and the West Riding of Yorkshire. He is director of music at Ilkley Secondary School and has been appointed head of the senior year and director of music at the new Ilkley Middle School.

THE PLAY (D.W.)

For some years now I have written plays for school productions and the question that people continue to ask me is 'How do you decide on a subject or plot?' My choice in this case, as in most of the others, was influenced by three main factors: the age-range of the children for whom I was writing, the various departments in the school who wished to be included in the production, and the audience for whom we were to play.

I felt that the age-range – from twelve to seventeen years – was by far the most important consideration. Whatever theme I chose it had to be one that would capture the imagination of all the children. Most children get a kick out of dressing up and performing on a stage, and I knew I would have no difficulty in finding a cast. But merely wanting to play was not enough; they needed characters they could understand and sympathize with. When one is dealing with 6-foot youths, and we had at least four boys over 6 feet who were keen and interested, one cannot present them with parts that are in any way soppy or effeminate. The characters had to be men through and through, the rougher the better. From three previous productions written for the school – *The Pearl*, a dance drama based on the book of the same name by Steinbeck, *Pericles*, adapted from the Shakespeare play, and *The Witch Boy*, from the American ballad of Barbara Allan and the Witch Boy – I had found that the most successfully played characters were simple fishermen, farmers and workmen. The interpretation of kings, princes and noblemen in *Pericles* the boys found much more difficult to handle. I was not too worried about the girls as they will usually tackle any type of part, the more emotional the better.

I carefully sifted through American and British musicals that had been written and produced during the last twenty years in the hope that I might find something that would appeal to the age group and thus give me a lead. I played selections of music from these shows to various classes of children to try and gauge their reactions, and found that *West Side Story* was by far the most popular. The reasons were obvious: it dealt with teenagers and some of their problems and the music was 'modern' – the type to which they were used to listening. This particular choice reminded me of a discussion I had had many years before. Someone had asked me, 'If you had to choose a Shakespearian tragedy to prepare with youth groups, which would be the easiest to do?' I said at the time that I felt that *Romeo and Juliet* was by far the most obvious choice, because the situations were the nearest of all the tragedies to their world and understanding.

The second factor in my choice of plot concerned the various departments that we hoped to involve in the production. The music and drama departments were obviously to be included, but to make effective use of our active dance–drama group we had to include in the script more than a few traditional dances, so that they could show their ability in creative movement. The group concerned contained few boys, and I felt that the boys who were willing to act and sing might draw the line if we asked them to dance. Also it did not necessarily follow that the best singers would be good at movement of this type. Nor could I expect all the dancers to be strong at singing. Thinking in terms of rehearsals I felt that the more the play could be split into definite sections, singers, dancers and straight actors, the better. When working with a cast of between sixty and seventy there is nothing worse than having big groups sitting about waiting for their turn to rehearse. So if it was possible to arrange something for the dance group that did not involve the main characters, something that could be rehearsed separately, it would make everything much easier.

Ideas for a plot were now forming. I decided to keep the location in Italy, as it offered opportunities for colour in both costumes and scenery. A small fishing village with its close-knit community, its constant battle with the sea and the fears for the safety of its men folk seemed a suitable background. To justify the use of gay, traditional costumes and national dances the idea of a local festival was introduced. From this idea came a play within a play, a festival mime or ballet, as a vehicle for the dance–drama group.

The contribution of the art and needlework department was not difficult to see. Having worked as designer and stage director for many years for a large amateur theatre, I was conscious from the start of the limitations, both financial and technical, of coping with a large number of elaborate costumes and many set changes. My aim was a colourful production with easily work-able set-changes and costumes that were within the scope of the needlework department.

Men's costumes can often be difficult if they are elaborate, involving considerable time and skill in the making. We avoided this pitfall and used simple fishermen's smocks, sweat shirts, waistcoats and dyed jeans. For the mime, with its limited number of characters, we could experiment with something more elaborate, involving the art department to a large extent.

Once the theme and location had been decided the actual writing came easily. Again I had the advantage of knowing the children well, having worked with them for a number of years. Apart from the opening chorus, 'Eventide', I did not write the songs in sequence, but had a rough idea from the start as to where they would fit into the plot. The whole of the first scene was used as an introduction to the setting, situation and characters. I deliber-ately lulled the audience into an atmosphere of peacefulness with the opening song to give more power and impact to the brawl which followed. This façade of peace and beauty, with its underlying viciousness, was again introduced into the conversation between the carter and Julia on her first entrance when she comments on the beauty of the cliffs and the sea and he tells her of the impending danger.

With the strangeness of the Italian names and the introduction of so many characters during the first scene, I deliberately left out the two comedy leads until scene 2. This scene at the village inn was very much a cover scene for the larger set-change, but it also served to lighten the atmosphere with the introduction of the comic song 'She should be dead', and to establish firmly in the audience's mind the parts played by the leading male characters. Scenes 3, 4 and 5 were straight developments of the various plot themes, the relationship between Julia and Philip, Raffio and Serena, and Aldo's plan to burn the boats and the subsequent ruin of the Montani family. The ballet–mime had no direct bearing upon the plot and was to be played straight after the interval, so that the break in the theme tied up with the natural interval break and did not split the story more than was necessary.

Act 2 was deliberately made much shorter than act 1. The action speeded up and the plot moved much more quickly. I felt that if the drama and tragedy were too long the children would not be able to sustain the atmosphere. Consequently the second inn scene was not just used for the audience to relax in after the tension and drama of the death scene, but also to give Julia and Marta a breathing space before the build-up in the final fight. On paper the last scene seems very brief and the change of heart between the two families too sudden. Some of the children remarked on this at the first reading, and I seriously thought of re-writing the whole scene at this point, but when we started rehearsing the moves and dramatic pauses the whole thing fell into shape and seemed quite natural.

For the story of the ballet–mime I wanted a story with a strong moral and dramatic quality, but not of a biblical theme. The idea of symbolic characters that could be used with great imagination – from the aspects of music, movement and costume – had strong appeal. The story of Pandora's box fitted the requirements and could be developed as we wished.

THE DANCE DRAMA

The story is split into two main scenes, 'The wedding' and 'The opening of the casket'. The first scene opens with peasants returning from the marriage ceremony of a young couple whom they carry shoulder-high in a gay, bright, noisy scene. The couple are placed centre stage and the peasants start to dance. The dance is traditional, with clapping hands and stamping feet. Unobserved by the crowd a tall, dark stranger enters high up behind; it is Lucifer the dark angel. He watches for a moment, then with a gesture freezes the whole crowd. Slowly he moves down and weaves his way amongst them until he reaches the bride. He is about to touch her when Michael, the fair angel, enters with a drawn sword. Lucifer springs back with a hiss of fear, and Michael, using the sword hilt as a cross, drives him out; then waving his sword above the crowd he restores them to normal. They continue to dance, oblivious of the danger that threatened.

With the end of the dance the young couple are led to the back, and their friends bring them gifts. Lucifer enters among the crowd, holding a mask to hide his evil face. He is followed by two men carrying a large casket. Lucifer leads the bride down to the casket. She comes slowly, and is over-awed by the gift from the unknown stranger. As she moves to open the casket Michael, with a flash of lightning, springs between the girl and the chest. He tears the mask from Lucifer's hand, and the crowd fall back in horror at the sight of his evil face. With a curse he leaves, and Michael gestures to the crowd to leave the box unopened. They go quietly and the scene closes.

The second scene takes place at the home of the young couple. The whole of the mime was performed in the town square, and the only props used were a bench and the casket. At the beginning of the scene the young girl enters and starts to sweep the floor. As she draws near to the casket she stops and listens; it is obvious she thinks she can hear something inside. At this point two women knock on the door and she hurries to let them in. They move about the room admiring this and that, but as they move near the casket the bride draws them to the bench and they sit. As they talk and admire the girl's ring it is obvious that one of the women is very curious about the casket. She rises and moves slowly towards it, unobserved by the other two. She stoops and listens, and the movement attracts the attention of the other two. The girl rises and draws them away. The other woman indicates that they must leave, and as they go out the bride waves from the door.

She returns to her broom, but is restless. She goes to the casket, listens, stops, puts her broom down and goes to the door. Opening it, she peers out to see if anyone is coming, then, standing with her back to the door, she stares at the casket. Slowly she moves to it and throws back the lid. Imme-diately the room is filled with the most discordant sounds and out springs the Spirit of War. The girl falls back in horror, and with hands over her ears rushes for the door. War, with a leap, intercepts her and draws her back to the centre of the room, then with great leaps dances around her as she cowers with fear. Next he draws from the casket the spirits of Pestilence, Poverty and Disease who join him in his triumphant dance. With the climax of the dance the four spirits leave the house and move out into the world.

For a moment all is quiet, then two more figures emerge slowly from the casket – Pride and Greed. They close the lid and slowly circle the form of the girl, then move in and lift her to her feet. They present her with a mirror and a jewelled necklace and she is drawn into a dance. First she mimics the moves of one spirit, then the other. Pride is slow and languid, Greed is quick and darting, snatching at things. The girl sits and preens herself in the mirror, until suddenly the whole stage is filled with noise. War and his companions drive in groups of peasants who fight and are driven to the ground. Lucifer enters triumphantly, and with big gestures directs his ser-

vants about the stage. Gradually the noise softens, the peasants drag themselves off and the girl runs to help her husband who lies wounded.

Michael enters quietly, and taking the girl by the hand leads her once more
to the casket. She draws back, but he gestures for her to open it. Slowly she
obeys, and Hope, with bound hands, rises out of the chest. With Michael's
sword the bride cuts the bonds and Hope moves to the still form of the
husband. With gentle hands she lifts his head and wipes the blood from his
face, then taking his hand and the hand of the girl she leads them out into
the world.

By the end of September the bulk of the writing was finished and I was able
to set about planning the year's programme. We aimed to finish all the
writing – book and music – by the end of the October holiday, and then to
start rehearsals. The dates of the production had been fixed for the end of
the first week in July. We planned to rehearse in separate groups until after
Easter, then pull the whole thing together with a final fortnight of full-day
rehearsals. The rest of the staff were agreeable to this if we did not encroach
upon lesson time earlier in the year. We knew that examinations would be
over by the third week in June and that problems of lesson interference
would not be great.

The printing of tickets, leaflets and programmes, along with publicity,
was organized by a group of fourth-form leavers and one member of staff –
this was treated as a year's project and started in October with the drawing
up of booking plans and the printing of tickets. Advance publicity was to
take the form of 2,000 throw-away leaflets. These were designed by the boys
and were made in the form of a folded book-marker which opened out to
show details of dates and booking arrangements. These were distributed
in the town. The programme was elaborate – an illustrated cover and six
pages. Much of this was planned before Christmas, and only the cast lists,
orchestra and acknowledgements were left until the last few weeks.

Although few of the principal parts were cast by this time, I felt that quite
a lot of preparatory work could be started on the costumes. Each girl in the
chorus would need one floor-length skirt, a working blouse, shawl and
apron. These aprons were to be of hessian or some rough material and be
floor-length to cover as much of the skirt as possible. For the festival scenes
the girls had a change of blouse; white this time, decorated with lace and
ribbons. Some had peasant head-dresses, some decorative white aprons,
and some shawls in bright colours with deep fringing. We decided it would
help the audience to recognize the two main families if we gave them individual colour schemes. One family wore blue, blue–greens and purples, and
the other family wore orange, reds, golds and browns.

4

When designing the ballet costumes I decided to put all the supernatural characters into masks. Most of the girls were doubling in the chorus, and I felt that a fifteen-minute interval was not sufficient time to do the elaborate make-up needed for these parts. Also, we have found that the children play far less selfconsciously when wearing a mask. The bases of the masks were made in felt and were used early in rehearsals to give the performers confidence in wearing them. We were prepared for many cast changes during the rehearsal months so most of the skirts were made on the large side so they could be adjusted, if necessary, to fit different people. The boys' costumes were left until last. We were fortunate in being able to borrow some waistcoats which we trimmed with braid and used for the tarantella dancers.

The sets – coloured sketches, ground plans and elevated drawings – were designed and made in the autumn, but most of the actual building had to wait until much nearer the time of performance, when we could use the stage. The school hall is used for physical education and the stage for a dining-room, so for most of the year we could only use them out of school time. By the end of October we were ready for the first rehearsals. The chorus, principals and orchestra met separately on three different nights to rehearse the songs and music. I rehearsed the speaking parts during the lunch-hour twice a week. I decided not to have a read-through with the whole cast at this point, for I felt the need to hear the various scenes a few times myself and make any minor adjustments before we were ready to listen to the piece as a whole.

We plotted each scene very slowly, cutting and altering as we went along. The children helped here, suggesting an alteration if they found a passage difficult to deliver. We had decided to duplicate all the girls' parts to give more girls an opportunity, and also to safeguard against illness on the night. As soon as possible we let the principals sing with the orchestra, and joined up the orchestra and dance with the mime, listening to the music on tape, and letting the children improvise on different ideas.

The rehearsals continued in this vein throughout the winter and early spring. By this time we had cast all of the principals and most of the smaller parts, and the costumes were well on the way. The chorus numbers fluctuated as children left school for various reasons, or acquired part-time jobs after school and so were unable to attend rehearsals. But, by the end of the Easter holidays we felt that we had at last settled to a cast that looked like being permanent. Rehearsals now having settled into a definite routine the children accepted the fact that they would be expected to stay at least three nights a week, and I was able to start work on various props that were small enough to be made in the art room.

At the end of May, we started work on the stage sets. The main set – the village square – was permanent. The whole of the back section was raised, in some places to a height of 6 feet. This gave extra space for grouping the large chorus. The other full stage set was built in two sections. These were double-sided flats and formed the wings of 'the harbour' and 'village square'. The whole of these sides revolved to hide the houses and form the cliff faces along the 'mountain road'. Because our stage apron was quite narrow, and I wanted to play with as little break as possible, we built out two aprons to each side of the orchestra. One was used mainly as the 'inn garden', and the other as the outside of the 'Donati house'. We kept these fairly simple so that they could be used as overflow areas of the main stage during the crowd scenes.

For the last two weeks we rehearsed all day and every day. I feel that these intensive rehearsals gave the children tremendous confidence and polish. For these last rehearsals we ran the production in the correct sequence, as the great difficulty with large casts is to make the back-stage movement smooth and easy to run.

Looking back after all the fun, excitement and hard work, I feel that all the children who worked on the production in any way – and there must have been nearly 150 – gained something they will always remember, a sense of achievement at having worked together in a team on something completely new which they helped to make a success.

THE MUSIC (H.W.J.)
The three factors which governed the choice of the play also applied to the choice of music. Most 'musicals', even today, use a style reminiscent of 1930 dance-band music, and those which do not, *West Side Story*, for example, are usually too difficult to manage without outside help, which we wished to avoid if possible. The solution was to provide home-made, bespoke music, tailored to the needs of our singers and instrumentalists, and this on a fairly large scale.

With regard to style, that which has the greatest appeal to teenagers is all too obvious, and although I do not object to the idea of a 'pop opera' it seemed unsuited to our story. We wished to suggest an Italian atmosphere, and after consulting one or two collections of European folk music I decided to use a style based upon Italian examples wherever possible. One cannot make everything sound like *Santa Lucia*, and the more sophisticated solos finally asserted their own character and style – which I find hard to define! As far as the available forces were concerned our first problem was one of surfeit. The school has 600 pupils on the roll, of whom some 100 are able to play the simpler hymn tunes at sight on an instrument. Since room had to be left for an audience we pruned our orchestra down to 25, of whom 3 played on stage in costume:

> four violins;
> two cellos;
> three descant recorders;
> two treble recorders;
> one flute;
> two clarinets;
> one trumpet;
> a percussion team of five, playing most instruments except timpani and xylophone;
> one accordian and two guitars who played as stage musicians in costume and make-up.

We had in addition the inevitable piano, which I do not like because of the 'Palm Court' effect. Casting around we found an old and battered American organ, which needed extensive repairs and was a semitone sharp. We tuned it by loading the reeds with plasticine, and devised a means of remote wind-supply with an old hose-pipe and vacuum cleaner. We then strapped a microphone inside and connected it up to our school public-address amplifier, an old but powerful model. On full volume the organ could be heard on the adjacent Ilkley Moor, nearly precipitating a fire-drill the first time it was used! This gave us a new and powerful sound to supplement the rather gentle tutti of the orchestra.

David Wildman has mentioned 6-foot youths. Not all of them were endowed with tuneful voices, but two could sing well enough for solo work, and several others had quite resonant voices, although on the whole we lacked bass quality. Of the 20 boys who offered their services 6 had what might be called 'atonal' voices and were passengers vocally, whilst 2 were still trebles and eventually sang with the altos. The remaining 12 ranged from bass through baritone, to what, for lack of a better word, we laughingly called tenor. It will be realized by music teachers that our bass line was precarious.

As was to be expected we had a plentiful supply of female vocal talent, and began with a chorus of 25 sopranos and an equal number of altos. Classification was done on the ability to sing a lower part rather than on voice quality. Rather disappointingly some altos dropped out before the performance, which spoilt the balance, although no one seemed to mind except me! Before auditioning for soloists I had taught one of the solo–chorus numbers to all our senior classes, and this was used as a test piece, together with a scale or two for range purposes. We then chose a team of soloists without allocating individual parts, and as each solo was written it was taught to the whole group, irrespective of voice, so that all the soloists knew each other's songs.

We were pleased to find that all those with known acting ability could also sing well, which saved us having to 'bend' the plot situations to enable indifferent actors to sing the solos. During these team rehearsals we were able to note the most suitable voices and temperaments for each part, and if necessary, to modify the solos to fit individuals. The practices took place each Monday, and after six weeks we allocated parts:

Aldo Donati (villain) – bass-baritone;
Riccardo Donati (tragic hero) – baritone;
Philip Montani (romantic lead) – baritone;
Sebastian (comedy role) – baritone-light voice;
Julia (romantic lead) – soprano;
Marta (tragic heroine) – soprano;
Rena (comedy role) – soprano;
Serena (small solo part) – soprano.

We were able to duplicate all four girls' parts, although one of the two Julias left before the production. Some of the solo dancers were also duplicated. Of the four-night run each double took two nights, singing in the chorus on the other nights. Of the four boys two could reach low G and the other two had baritone ranges, one of whom – the comedian – dropped out subsequently and had to be replaced by an immature voice, creating certain problems which are discussed later. For the chorus we were dependent upon bass quality from the soloists who often had to sing from the wings.

As the words of each song were completed they were given to me together with suggestions of mood and dramatic context. Many of the songs were written before the play text was completed, and some of them were developed or modified as the story unfolded – chorus sections added, reprises arranged and so on – some were adjusted to fit the soloists once these had been determined. For the ballet music I worked from a scenario, the details of which have already been given, and found this to be the most exciting part of the music writing.

Those who have tried their hand at writing music for schoolchildren will know that there is more to it than thinking up a tune for a set of words. It may be of help to those who have not done so to know the sequence I followed. There are various factors to consider before trying out actual tunes.

First, the stage character of the singer; villains are often basses, heroes tenors. Second, the style of music required by plot background, in this case nineteenth-century Italian; one or two genuine Italian folk tunes were used, and the style of others was imitated. The third consideration is choice of key, a rather complex matter, best approached when the head is clear. Trumpets and clarinets add two sharps to any key in which the non-transposing instruments play. This doesn't rule out the sharp keys for them, of course, but the parts must be made easier if a harder key is chosen. Four sharps was the limit for our clarinets and more than the limit for our trumpet. The practical limit for recorders is two sharps or flats, although they can manage others as occasional accidentals. Violins have a slight bias towards sharp keys, although our players were good enough for this to be ignored. The easiest keys will therefore be F and C major, and much of our purely instrumental music was in these two keys, where a key was identifiable, with D minor as an easy alternative.

With song forms there is a further factor to consider. The range of simple songs is usually one of two types, either from *soh* to *soh*, or *doh* to *doh* of any given key, corresponding roughly to the plagal and authentic forms of the old modal scales. Since the range of the average voice is approximately an octave plus three notes, the best keys for the two melodic types are D and G (major or minor) or C and F. As much of the instrumental music was to use C and F, for the sake of contrast the vocal music tended to use D and G.

The vocal range of teenage boys imposes limits on songs written for them. Our boys' voices fell into three rough (some were very rough) types. There were the fifth formers, 6-feet tall and embryonic basses, with a range from low G to middle D or E; more numerous were the baritones with an effective range of about one octave below treble voices – C to E. The third group were the immatures, or in-betweens, to whom I have already referred as tenors. Their range was about G below middle C to G above, a most awkward range for class-work. Incidentally, a quite impressive effect can be obtained by putting down the pitch of a song by a fourth or so and asking the girls to sing low down in unison with these boys. This is usually regarded as a great joke, but seems to work nevertheless.

Our boy soloists started out as one bass and three baritones, but ended up as one bass, two baritones and an immature. Only the latter needed his solos modified. The chorus parts were largely written for baritone range and would be rather high for adult basses. They contained alternative notes for the low basses or high immatures, but as these led to confusion their value was questionable. Writing for the girls was easier since they have a wider pitch range and more stable voices. At fifteen there are very few real altos, so the alto part was a second soprano. The first sopranos had to sing F♯ and G at times, and finished the finale on a magnificent high B♭. They often complain that an F is too high in the classroom, so it would seem that costumes and make-up do more for the voice than volumes of *bel canto* exercises.

It was important to see that the climaxes came in the resonant part of the soloists's voice, and that the accompaniment gave the singer help without obscuring the words, a good rhythmic foundation being most essential. When I felt I had an effective melody I added an accompaniment of two staves, with suggestions for orchestration. For the soloists we used a smaller group consisting of strings, clarinets and flute. This also made rehearsing much easier. In the first violin copy I placed many vocal cues and tunes so that the leader could help the singer if necessary. The organist had most of the score condensed on to three staves, considerable use being made of coloured felt pens to distinguish between the parts. This was in the case of breakdowns or absences, and although it involved much extra copying was a valuable form of insurance. It also meant that I could conduct from the organ if the organist was absent. Just to tie matters up completely, the organist, a part-time music teacher on our staff, was prepared to direct if I collapsed on the rostrum!

EXAMPLES OF VOCAL MUSIC

The first example is part of the opening chorus which was sung by the boy and girl trebles, the fishermen being out in the boats. The chorus started after a prologue, and had a short introduction featuring a bell chiming six o'clock. The singers came on in groups, and after two verses there was stage action followed by a reprise in which dancers took part. The tune is based on an Italian folk tune called 'Hark the Cock Crows' – which is rather odd, as our chorus was called 'Eventide'.

The next two excerpts, Examples 2 and 3, are from a duet for bass and baritone. The father, Aldo (6-foot bass), is exhorting his son Riccardo to help him in a plan to burn the boats of the rival family. Riccardo calls the plan foolish and dangerous. The dialogue was in the form A B B A B. 'A' was Aldo's first exhortation, bass range A to A in pitch, key D minor. 'B' was a tune in D major, baritone range D to D, first used by Aldo to describe his plan, then by Riccardo to express his contempt for it. Aldo repeats his first bass theme – 'A' – then finally both 'B' versions are sung together. To avoid obscuring the different sets of words the 'B' tune was sung in canon, using the same accompaniment. Neither of the boys had any difficulty with it, the bass being sixteen and the baritone fifteen. Since Aldo's first words are 'Maybe I'm wrong, but I feel that we'll win this fight', I gave him a diminished chord to open on, suggesting menace, with a dash of uncertainty. A boys' chorus sang the song to end the scene.

EXAMPLE I

EXAMPLE 2

I referred earlier to difficulties with immature boys' voices. A part in question was that of Sebastian, a weedy, henpecked husband, who had a comedy solo and a duet with Rena his wife. We were able to duplicate Rena, having two excellent comedy actresses with generous figures and voices to match. Sebastian was more difficult; little weedy boys often have little weedy voices, and we needed one who could be heard. We found one with almost a baritone range, and I provided him with a solo in G minor which

EXAMPLE 3

had a range of D to D, hoping that he would develop the extra tone or so during the nine months before production. His voice remained obstinately the same until about two months before our opening, and just as he began to sing the part he had to leave. By good luck we discovered a natural clown to take over the part, but he was definitely in the immature category, although he was uninhibited about his singing and could make himself heard. The solution was to write him a new line which fitted the existing chorus and orchestra parts. Example 4 shows the beginning of his song which is a mock funeral dirge for his wife. The upper vocal line is the later Sebastian, the double treble clef indicating a pitch one octave lower.

EXAMPLE 4

The full choruses were mostly scored for soprano, alto and bass, and much time was spent trying to improve the singing of the more precarious basses. As music teachers will guess, the most rich and resonant bass proved to be totally unco-ordinated aurally, and finally had to be silenced, with instructions to mime the choruses in 'pop star' fashion. Since the great vice of teenage baritones is to desert their part for that of the sopranos one octave lower, I tried wherever possible to give them counterpoint in both word and music, which makes for less confusion with the soprano part. A successful example is shown in the chorus of 'Italy' (Example 5), perhaps the most popular number of all. It included a very effective dance from some of the girls, whilst guitar and accordian played onstage.

EXAMPLE 5

The song which gave me the greatest personal pleasure was a long aria for two girls, Julia and Marta, which included a duet section. Marta has just lost her lover, Riccardo, stabbed whilst intervening in a quarrel. She sings a lament, 'I knew his love', which changes to a condemnation of her friend, whom she blames for the tragedy. Julia intervenes, pleading with Marta not to be bitter, and the climax of the song comes as they combine in short, dramatic phrases, finally singing the simple, sweeping tune of the last verse which brings the scene to a close. All three girls involved acted and sang with great feeling and sincerity, making this a moving experience for all who heard it. Example 6 shows the climax of the song.

The final chorus was ushered in by a solo from Julia, and Example 7a shows an orchestral texture which was difficult for the soloist. The sliding

EXAMPLE 6

harmony of the accompaniment sounded fine on the piano, an instrument which is a congenial companion for any singer. The same kind of accompaniment from an orchestra can become a morass in which the singer flounders helplessly. With practice, both Julia and the orchestra managed it very well, including the change of mood shown in this example.

THE INSTRUMENTAL MUSIC

Our school orchestra normally meets once a week and is constantly growing in size, partly because of the excellent service of peripatetic instrumental teachers provided by the local education authority. Most of the instruments are bought from school funds, although several players own their own. The orchestra started four years ago as a dozen descant recorders and two violins, and at the time of writing has over thirty members. We have a plentiful supply of recorder players as all first- and second-form pupils learn to play in class music lessons.

EXAMPLE 7a

EXAMPLE 7b

(+ gradual addition of woodwind and percussion)

Rehearsals involved some of our members on three evenings of the week, and as our school buildings are a mile apart, this meant much trudging to and fro in all weathers. Since the music department is in one building and the main hall in another we had much transporting of equipment to do, this being the most irksome of many handicaps. When planning the ballet music we had experimental sessions in which I asked the players to suggest certain moods or ideas by improvising and finding new sounds, and some of these ideas were incorporated in the score, much to everyone's delight.

For the ballet music I was given a scenario with indications of mood and duration of episodes and had a free hand to provide whatever music I thought fit. As a general principle it was decided to use fairly orthodox, concordant music for the human element, but anything supernatural was to be accompanied by definitely weird sounds, and to this end our percussion section enlarged its armoury with a gong, two whips (hinged boards), temple blocks and siren whistles. Most of the small 'kitchen' equipment was hung on a dexion frame which enabled two or three players to use the same instrument. The first task after composing was to make a piano tape-recording of the whole ballet so that it could be choreographed. This was difficult to manage due to the sounds involved, but we could not wait until the orchestra has learned the music. Various modifications were made during choreography (which was also done at experimental sessions with the dancers), and the final version was practised separately by dancers and orchestra until ready for joint rehearsals; these began about a month before opening night.

The first formal dance was a tarantella, danced by the wedding guests; a simple tune over a drone-bass was used. When Lucifer enters he has his theme or leitmotif in the Wagnerian manner. This theme was a descending whole-tone scale of four notes and was used whenever Lucifer entered. The three examples below show the tarantella theme (Example 8), Lucifer's entry theme used in the tarantella (Example 9), and Lucifer's entry theme used in the 'Gift bringing' music (Example 10).

EXAMPLE 8

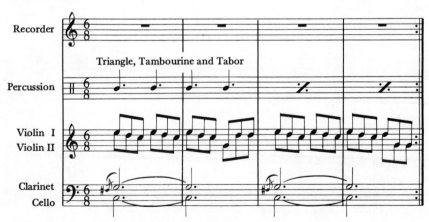

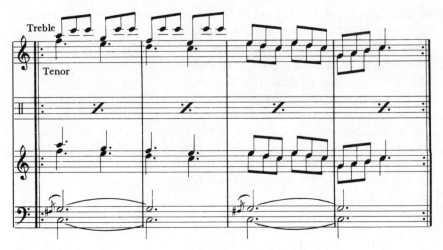

EXAMPLE 9

EXAMPLE 10

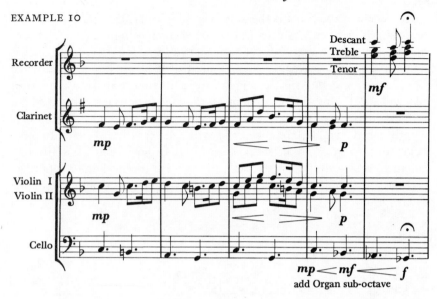

Lucifer's theme was used as the basis for improvisation on the two occasions when he made a rapid and undignified exit. Example 11 shows his first exit after his confrontation with the angel, rather in the style of cat facing dog.

EXAMPLE 11

In scene 2 of the ballet is the long 'sweeping' episode, during which the bride shows great curiosity about the noises coming from Lucifer's casket, finally opening the lid, with the well-known disastrous consequences for humanity. For the 'sweeping' theme I used an Italian folk tune called 'The Grasshopper and the Ant', adding a further section to make it a metrical sixteen bars. The music consisted of a series of variations interrupted by the listening episodes. During these episodes we used a sound made up of a wire-brushed cymbal, tremolo cello with glissando and violin tremolo below the bridge. The instructions to the remaining cello aroused much comment and were interpreted in various ways by the humorists of the orchestra. Example 12 shows part of the 'sweeping' tune and one of the interruptions.

EXAMPLE 12

Six evil spirits were to leave the casket, four themes being needed for them as follows (see Example 13): War; Pestilence, Poverty and Disease; Pride; Greed. The whips in the Greed theme were very successful. Whips are easily made by hingeing two flat pieces of wood together and adding handles.

A little later in the ballet all the spirits come on together, directed by Lucifer with imperious gestures. The themes of the spirits are combined with that of Lucifer in a noisy climax – see Example 14 – where our eighty-year-old reed organ really came into its own.

EXAMPLE 13

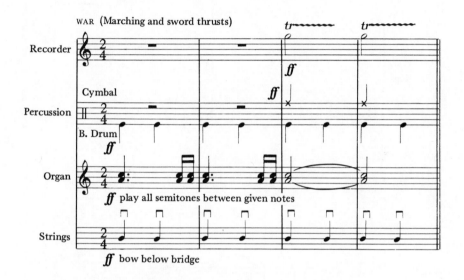

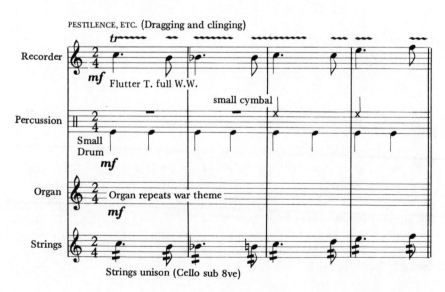

The examples of our music are not given to show how well it was written, but rather to show the simple methods we used. I imagine that a student of composition might wince at my score, but such people rarely have to deal with secondary modern schoolchildren. I have a folk song suite for school orchestras, published by a reputable music firm, the last movement of which involves descant and treble recorders in a 6/8 presto in A major. The composer obviously had little experience of teaching children to play the recorder, but he could have consulted a practising teacher about his work!

The production brought out unsuspected qualities in many pupils. Seniors, boys and girls, took charge of both dramatic and musical sectional

EXAMPLE 14

practices. A girl with a speech defect delighted us all with beautiful articulation in singing and dialogue. The fourth-year leavers class produced a splendid programme, and made for the orchestra a set of illuminated music rests to fit on our stands. The junior art section made curtains for the orchestra pit, decorated with *appliqué* instruments. There has been a notable increase of interest in modern works when they are presented in music lessons, whilst an almost professional attitude is taken towards operatic recordings. The local operatic society has begun to recruit our soloists, who will perhaps encourage the society to a more adventurous choice than *Goodnight Vienna* for its future productions.

Realism and fantasy

ROBERT THOMSON and MALCOLM JOHN

In young children the world of reality and the world of fastasy often intermingle. But eleven- to fourteen-year-old children, through physiological processes and the demands of adult society, tend not to externalize their fantasies – unless it be through drama and social dance. Previously spontaneous activities are turned inwards and reading, listening and watching take the place of acting and doing. In the following two works young people play 'themselves'. At the same time they are called upon to extend their imagination into the world of children's games in the first play, and a creative dream-state in the second.

Robert Thomson is a graduate of York University. He has studied at the New College of Speech and Drama and holds Diplomas in Dramatic Art from London University and the Royal Academy of Music. He has produced plays at the Arts Centre in York, and teaches at Wetherby High School.

Malcolm John read music at Melbourne University, is a diplomate of Juilliard School of Music, New York, and has completed three years' research in children's music drama at York University. He has taught in primary and secondary schools, and lectures at Salisbury Teachers' College, South Australia.

'NOT WITH A BANG' (R.T.)
I wrote *Not with a Bang* because I believe that participation in dramatic productions is both educative and enjoyable. Drama can play a great part in promoting a child's awareness of himself and others. He is encouraged to co-operate rather than compete, to develop his skills for the benefit of the group as well as for his own satisfaction. Most of all, he is encouraged to use his imagination to extend and comprehend his experience of the world.

Although I wrote the play with one particular group of children in mind I hoped to make it adaptable to the requirements of any other group that might come to perform it. As far as possible I tried to distribute the parts evenly so that no child would be given unfair prominence over the others. Also, I wished to give every child something to say or do so that everyone would be actively involved throughout. Finally, I tried to ensure that the play could be performed with the minimum of scenery and properties.

This was to give plenty of scope for the producer who has the best facilities at hand, while making the play available for effective classroom performance. Because of this I had to avoid any situation which might necessitate the use of elaborate costumes. The logical answer to these limitations was a play involving a crowd of children in old or ragged clothes, and set against an indeterminate background.

Fortunately I was reminded of a dance drama based upon Brecht's 'Children's Crusade 1939', which I had seen performed by drama students some years previously. As a copy of the poem was not at hand I decided to strike out on my own, setting the scene in a bleak and war-weary country. From the first image of the ragged pathetic child standing alone amongst the desolation, the play almost began to write itself. As it developed, I felt that the theme was in danger of being too doleful, and so, almost wilfully, I turned the tables by introducing a fantasy scene. This was to give comic relief whilst reminding the audience of the cause of the children's distress. As well as showing the tragic results of war, the play – particularly the comic scene – demonstrates how children might come to terms with life through acting out situations in play.

Of course there are weaknesses of plot, and the ending is unashamedly *deus ex machina*; however, I prefer to let the play stand as written. If children can feel comfortable inside the shaky structure I created for *Not with a Bang* and enjoy the experience of acting and singing with others, then I consider my play successful.

STORY AND MUSIC (M.J.)

It was through being involved as leaders in York Children's Theatre Workshop every Saturday morning that Robert Thomson and I decided – as an outlet for our own interests as well as an aim for the eleven- and twelve-year-old children – to write a short music drama involving some twenty to thirty volunteers. We were fortunate in three respects: the children appeared keen on the story and the possibility of a performance; Gabriel Barnfield, a founder-member of the workshop agreed to be the producer; and through the encouragement of Peter Aston, the composer, the play was included in the 1968 Harrogate Festival of Arts and Sciences. The fact that the performances were arranged for the school holiday period – August – did not make the task of recruiting the cast any easier. However, twenty girls and boys of different abilities and backgrounds – and whom I had no intention of eliminating on the grounds of poor vocal technique – began rehearsals after Easter. Some of the children had sung very little either at home or at school, but all except three had quite clear voices which gained in confidence and authority as we progressed.

The script, mainly in verse form, lent itself to four different treatments from the point of view of setting it to music, and these in turn blended with or contrasted with each other, according to the particular scene or situation. These were:

(1) straight prose;
(2) prose or verse with background music;
(3) verse in a definite rhythm, with and without music;
(4) song – mainly unison, but occasionally in two parts.

The prose passages were not 'dialogue' as such, but brief narrative- or rest-points between the tense or more active passages. As the whole play only took twenty-five minutes to perform I was determined that the musical ideas should match the three-part dramatic structure, and that the work should be a unified and integrated whole. To this end I used – only half consciously – an opening fragment of melody, or theme, which spawned a variety of different patterns of melody for several of the subsequent songs. This is a perfectly natural compositional process used by all composers within their own chosen style. Thus in the middle comical fantasy, the opening theme is changed (inverted, transposed, lengthened), and becomes light-hearted and frivolous. With the return of reality the first fragments are reiterated and intensified, until the final release of tension and a re-awakening of hope in the last few minutes.

There were six soloists – three boys and three girls – and no minor roles. Having experienced some mediocre pit orchestras in school productions I was determined that nothing should stand – literally and figuratively – between the players on stage and their audience, without whom the essence of the drama would be only half realized. Therefore I kept the orchestra to a minimum but aimed for maximum use of the instrumental colour available from the meagre resources. So our orchestra consisted of a clarinet and two players on percussion, thus allowing the small voices to come through. The three instrumentalists sat to the side-front of the stage (in this case of the hall/dining-room type) leaving maximum contact of the actors with the audience. Although we had the services of a clarinet teacher and two older students for the seven or eight percussion instruments I purposely kept the technical demands of both parts well within the reach of fifth-grade music standards.

There were often passages when a soloist or the chorus would have to supply the extra strand of melody to existing single, double or triple layers of sound, and there were moments when, for the dramatic effect, pitch was superimposed with shouts, noises and screams. This latter state of affairs was not so apparent on paper, but as is so often the case with dramatic scenes in rehearsal the real involvement with the story brought in new

Realism and fantasy   63

In staging – keep simple – use lighting + things effectively

dimensions to an otherwise purely musical concept. In both instances I was not a little surprised at how confidently certain dissonances – as part of the overall style – were held.

Although an 'arena' performance may have been desirable – and almost certainly may have been used in the classroom situation – certain facts militated against this approach in the production. It was to be a public performance, in surroundings with which we were not familiar, and we wished to make use of available lighting effects which were to be found only behind the proscenium arch. In spite of the imposed environment and the fourth wall, the players never lost sight of their own sense of interaction as characters within the drama, and there was certainly never any 'playing up' to the audience. The scenery was simple but not unrealistic. A crumbling corner of a ruined building was represented in the foreground by two 11-feet

EXAMPLE I

keep scenery simple

flats attached at right angles – one containing an existing 'window' hole – and surrounding a double height of 1-foot and 2-foot rostra. Tiles of 1-foot Polystyrene were cut and pasted to the edges of the upright flats; larger chunks of the same type of material formed the extended, broken base of the walls of what could have been a bombed-out warehouse. With two small sides of an old fruit box nailed across the open window, and appropriate browns, greens and blacks covering the structure, it was seen in stark perspective against a mass of nailed criss-cross lengths of box wood representing the distant, destroyed skyline of a town. In the lighting changes of two – upper and lower – cyclorama battens plus eight spots – one green for the ogre – and one overhead batten for warmer tones, a great variety was obtained, reflecting the general moods of the play, although the changes wrought were infrequent and only at crucial moments. As there was a considerable amount of movement in the drama – seeking, building, marching and washing clothes – most of the stage area was left bare.

The play begins in darkness, before dawn. To the long, sustained clarinet 'A' a ragged group are discovered huddling together for warmth (see Example 1).

Soon Joseph sings his plaintive song; this returns near the end but with different words:

> A town was here where the dogs dig for bones;
> And all I have to eat is a dry crust of bread.
> Soon Winter will be here, but I have no warmth,
> And there is no shelter to cover my head.

The others murmur in ostinato underneath (see Example 2).

EXAMPLE 2

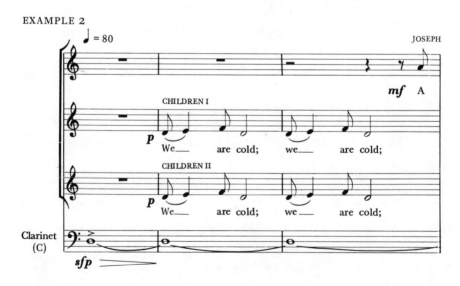

town was here where the dogs dig for bones,

we ___ are cold; we ___ are cold;

we ___ are cold; we ___ are cold;

They then express their frustration and anger in jagged verse. Julie becomes concerned for the younger children (Example 3).

Tomás is very hungry and says so, while the others turn on him for being so selfish. They become lost in their misery once more. Suddenly Joseph suggests that they build a shelter out of the rubble. This is taken up immediately and as they scatter around the dump looking for and finding old doors, string, and nails (mimed), their mood becomes lively. The xylophone

EXAMPLE 3

JULIE

Slowly

mf What can we do? The

young ones are hun-gry, and we have not ea-ten for

Clarinet (C)

Alto Glockenspiel

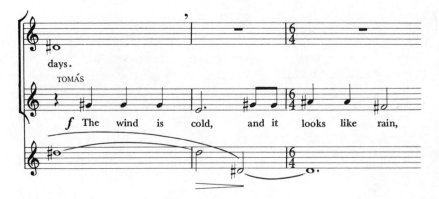

takes the place of the big drum, and the rhythms take on a syncopated character. Having built their shelter they sit in it (on the rostra between the old walls) and sing their song of achievement (Example 4).

Then Tomás does go off with one of the others looking for his 'big steak pie' while the others rummage around on stage (Example 5).

EXAMPLE 4

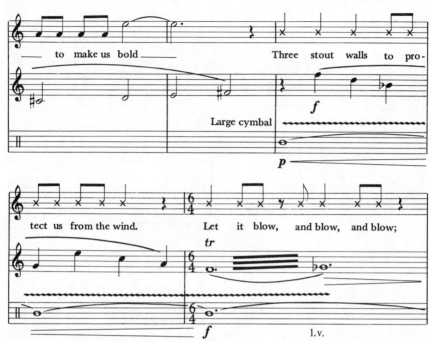

They soon tire of this and the little ones (played by shorter members of the cast) persuade Peter to tell them a story. The fantasy section begins. Telling a story to children – and for that matter adults – must be one of the oldest means of entertainment known; certainly a very basic one. The children react immediately to the story and 'live it'. The boys become soldiers and the girls turn into washerwomen, while one boy becomes Ogre Bill, the terrible tyrant of Williamstown. The atmosphere changes as if by

EXAMPLE 5

EXAMPLE 6

magic; there is laughter and anticipation. The soldiers assemble carrying sticks for guns and making drumming sounds with their lips as they march about very confidently. Having saluted their tyrant the boys dissolve quietly into the background, still miming movement but not attracting the focus of attention. The girls now jump up and become breezy washerwomen. Example 6 shows the linking of narration, by way of the soldiers' marching rhythm and the pitch given on the glockenspiel.

The ogre decides he wants to inspect his men.

> PETER: One Summer morn', at half past ten
> The ogre, he decided to inspect his men.
> Took a shiny helmet and a sword from his box,
>   (*mimed in exaggerated fashion*)
> But found to his horror he had no clean socks!

> OGRE BILL: Send for the captain of the guard!
> You'll find him playing marbles in the yard.
> Send him my best regard,
> And tell him to come at once!
>   (*a soldier salutes and dashes off*)

The ogre's instrument is the large cymbal, and it reflects his growing anger. The captain (Joseph or one of the others) comes and suggests that he get the washerwomen to clean his socks. But they have already stated that these are the only things they will *not* wash. Ogre Bill orders his army to burn down the houses, and pull down their lines. This they proceed to do amid much fear and trembling; the slow march of the army being particularly menacing as it introduces tuned timpani (2) for the first time. However, during the sacking of the 'washing' the ogre begins to sneeze – very obvious runs on the clarinet – and when questioned as to what is wrong, replies:

> OGRE BILL: Carry me back to my castle on the hill.
> Yes, it's chicken pox, and flu, and it's a chill.
> I am sure I will die, so back to home I'll fly;
> It's enough to make me cry, so I will.
>   (*takes out a big, red handkerchief*)

Little Ingrid moves over to him and, tugging gently at the cuff of his ragged jacket, says:

> INGRID: Do not cry, wicked ogre, do not cry.
> We will wash your socks; we will scrub your socks.
> ALL GIRLS: And maybe even hang them out to dry.

The soldiers – who have been blown over by the last final sneeze – begin to rise. The washerwomen tune and the building tune are heard in free

EXAMPLE 7

juxtaposition as Ogre Bill repents and invites them all to a feast ... The mood changes abruptly. Faces change, lighting reverts to the cold starkness of the opening scene. The doleful rising moan is heard on the clarinet together with the rattle of the sticks (claves). The rising minor third ostinato is heard once more, reinforced by clarinet and timpani (see Example 7).

The sound of Tomás and his old drum is heard in the distance. They listen and brighten a little. Finally he arrives with a big bag full of food.

> ALL: (*same tune as when searching earlier on*)
> Come listen to the drum, the drum, the drum,
>   and dance and sing.
> Come taste the food, the food, the food,
>   come taste the food.
> There's lots for me and more for you,
> There'll even be some food left over too.

They munch away, humming a previous happy tune as they are issued in turn with food from the deep bag. At last Tomás produces his pie and holds it aloft for all to see:

ALL: Yes a most enormous, quite fantastic, truly gigantic, even elephantic, muscle-giving reason-for-living Pie. (*long held 'C' chord, and busy instruments*)

'A TIME FOR DICÉ' – POP OPERA (M.J.)

It is a paradox that these two words pop and opera should be linked together at all, but what prompted the creation of this work was a concern for the adolescent – fourteen to sixteen years old – and his or her education in the broadest sense. The drama came first, but because of the substance of the drama (an episode in the lives of a pop group) a musical setting for these events and the final tragedy seemed only appropriate. There was certainly nothing 'gimmicky' about the writing of either the words or the music, and it is strange that some teachers would write pop style music with a 'let's-get-it-out-of-their-systems-and-clear-their-minds-of-this-rubbish' approach, and treat the whole matter as a farce rather than make an attempt at real dramatic communication with their third- and fourth-form children. By the time these children reach the fifth and sixth form such an opportunity has disappeared, for they are now, for the most part, young adults, and have much more sophisticated and complex views about life and would not like to appear 'ridiculous' in the eyes of their fellow pupils.

It was in such a spirit of communication and participation and a desire that there should be a true dramatic experience involving the forty boys and girls – about equally divided – who volunteered to participate that I let myself go and wrote a short play using verse and dialogue loosely based upon the ancient Greek legend of Orpheus. Carrying the spirit of pop into the structure of the drama itself I used anagrams of the names of the original hero and underworld deities as modern names for the small town pop group and all but three of the other parts. For example, Orpheus the musician becomes Art Shoupré the lead guitar, while Charon, ferryman on the underground river Styx becomes Ron Char the bass guitar player, and the Styx river became Sticks Revri the drummer. In creating the actual plot I kept five points in mind:

(1) To include as much movement, dancing, and colour as possible, and to have the verses both danced and sung at the same time;

(2) to keep to a simple A B A structure, the main climax occurring at the closing of B, and to confine the action to one act, keeping it as fluent as possible;

(3) to realize the essence of the characters concerned rather than try as an adult to use slick expressions in vogue amongst teenagers today. If necessary, anything of this nature can be added in rehearsal by the young actors themselves;

(4) to direct the whole play toward the climax, and yet to allow the singing to be enjoyable for its own sake, with a hint – in the words and music of the solos and choruses – of their place in the overall scheme of things;

(5) to allow a complete scene to be created from scratch by the children

from experimentation and improvisation, using a variety of sound sources and any available equipment.

With these points in mind, six scenes were organized as follows.

Scene 1: a village hall or youth club Friday night dance. Introduction of the group (4 to 6 players and singer). Entry of Charlie Levid, a cunning 'agent' from the city, and his girl Jenny Dicé (rhymes with Euridice), plus two of his cronies, Willy and Wontie. He flatters the group and invites them to an audition.

Scene 2: Levid's apartment, high up in a big block of flats; wide, loosely-hanging curtains are mid-stage through which is revealed the Hades scene later on. The cleaning woman comments upon the ways of the world and sings a traditional Suffolk ballad – linked by innuendo to the plot – then Levid's two cronies enter. Rather odd and humorous situations develop, and this scene helps to set the evil and at times pathetic background against which the main protagonists move.

Scene 3: Jenny and Art, attracted to each other by now, enter the flat. It is later in the same day and they are the first back from the recording session. They express their feelings in a duet, then the others of the group enter. The Orpheus theme is alluded to in conversation, and finally, Levid, Willy and Wontie appear. The celebrations begin with a song, then the drugged drinks are passed around. As they all succumb to the power of the drug the Hades scene is revealed.

Scene 4: figures appear and reappear in fantastic costume while weird music and sounds are heard throughout the hall. Expressive dance drama depicting Jenny's 'falling from life' a second time is enacted, while Art, in a dream state, pleads with her to return. The dream ends, and slowly all recover consciousness. Jenny is discovered dead on the couch. Ron, Sticks and Sarah are too shocked to interrupt Levid and his friends as they sneak out a back way. (Including *Scene 5*).

Scene 6: back in the village hall some three weeks later the group are playing again, and it is only in the context of what has taken place that Sarah's song, 'Yesterday', can be fully understood. The chorus finally sing their song 'Now', which expresses a certain joy in simply being alive, and the play ends.

We had an hour and a half on Wednesday afternoons for about ten weeks of the spring term in which to prepare the production. This time was normally a free activities afternoon and four young and enthusiastic members of staff volunteered to give of their time and skills. Not having the pressures of external examinations, the fourth-form children were able to become completely involved in the drama. Having spent about three or four months writing, copying and typing the work, and preparing enough full-scores, chorus parts and libretti for the staff and forty children, we began the first rehearsal with a run through the main choruses. I had explained the plot and demonstrated some of the music during the previous term, and auditions had been held for the girls to keep the numbers down. Both schools have a strong musical life, and the fifth and sixth forms frequently come together for choral and orchestral concerts; however, for the fourth forms being together under these circumstances was something of a novelty. The schools are about a mile and a half apart, but the boys found no difficulty in walking three miles for a short rehearsal. The girls had written and performed a Halloween play when in the third form and were keen for wider participation in the same medium. The boys had done little drama before, although during the previous two years the first- and second-form boys had all taken an active part in creating their own music dramas, the subjects of the plots ranging from Guy Fawkes to space travel and guerilla warfare, some being ballad operas, others works encompassing a great variety of sounds, musical and otherwise.

The second rehearsal was spent in completing the chorus parts and running over the music of the previous week. Although there was much unison singing the girls did at times split up into three parts, while the boys, because of the relative immaturity of their voices, gained confidence by keeping to unison (light baritone range) with occasional excursions into two parts. There was also much canonic and imitative division into 'high' girls and boys against 'low' girls and boys. One hour on Friday evenings was set aside for the principals' singing rehearsal. The chorus and solo singing in the first and last scenes was accompanied by the pop group (boys in this case), consisting of lead guitar, rhythm guitar, bass guitar, organ and drums. Their vested interest in the opera was an added incentive for them to begin to observe some subtler shades of dynamic and to seek a variety of tone with which they were unfamiliar – particularly when accompanying soloists – and their reading of music was forced to become more fluent.

The third week was divided between a creative movement session in the gymnasium – the first for the boys, and also fairly new to the girls – and a discussion of the main characters, from a thoughtful and subjective point of view, by the principals. We also read through the whole script while I briefly suggested the type of person which I had had in mind for each part. The average age of the group in the play is about nineteen, and the ages of Levid and his cronies range between thirty-eight and fifty. The woman is elderly and Jenny is young. They were asked to have their dialogue learnt by the next week, and the group and chorus joined forces for the last half-hour and sang the first chorus, 'I wish', from memory (see Example 8).

From a vocal point of view the children sang in a natural manner, and there was never any attempt to imitate the more forced and crude tone of some pop singers, as this would have destroyed the clear quality of their immature voices. If anything, emphasis was placed upon clarity of attack and enunciation of words – as in a normal choral situation – and, because of stimulating rhythmic syncopation and a lightness of style, the children found this music quite easy to learn. The problem of 'balance' between the powerful electric guitars, organ and drums and the singers (who had no amplification) was a real one, and had to be handled tactfully but firmly.

EXAMPLE 8

The group was made aware of its part in the whole production and soon realized that they had to turn down their volume at certain times so that the singers could be heard! At least they had the means of doing this and of producing some sensitive and quite beautiful sounds, whereas with the usual 'pit orchestra' young singers inevitably have some difficulty in penetrating the sound barrier – particularly if the players are heavy-handed.

In the solos and small ensemble work I tended to stress dynamic shading and variety in the playing and singing rather than the solid beat and exuberance which was the hall-mark of the chorus numbers. Sarah, the singer in the group, sings 'Yesterday' which demonstrates this approach (see Example 9).

Apart from a basic knowledge of keys, chords and simple progressions (and a desire to doodle at the keyboard) the main requirement to write for such a combination of instruments seems to be the ability to listen carefully to the hundreds of sounds bursting from the pop radio sessions, to analyse the means whereby these sounds are produced, to discard that which is boring and unintelligible (most of it) and to recreate in your own style and with the utmost simplicity straightforward songs (structurally) with words which express aspects of that highly charged feeling and enthusiasm which are part of the lives of the children you teach and observe for most of your

EXAMPLE 9

Organ and Guitar as for voices

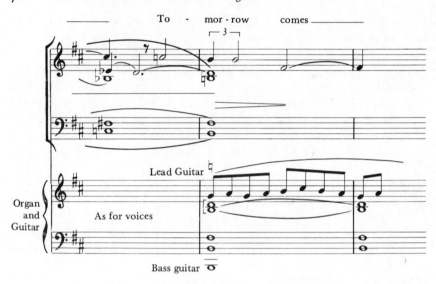

working life. It is also essential to know the limitations of the players for whom you are writing. For example, the lead guitar possessed a good memory and an interest in new tone colours; both rhythm guitar and organist could read very well, while the bass guitar read only the treble clef and had to really work at deciphering some of the more chromatic passages. We had to borrow a good set of drums, and our drummer's inventive powers increased rapidly as rehearsals progressed. Naturally there were passages in the score for improvisation, but these were sudden 'rips' of two or three bars rather than long sections. 'Now' (see Example 10) is an example of a more light-hearted style, and gives some indication of the balance of forces mentioned above.

EXAMPLE 10

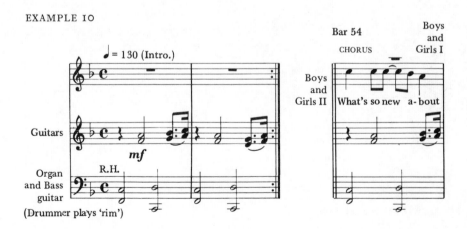

Charlie Levid sings an egotistical song – 'What a shame' – with comments from principals and chorus. In this there is a strict economy of material, and a ground bass – stemming from the first theme – forms the basis of the longer second half of the song, with voices entering one by one as the soloists sum up the situation. It is by altering rhythm and moving the descending progressions up a tone, from D to E, that the obvious mood contrast is affected (see Example 11). One moves from a feeling of good-humoured boasting to sinister speculation with simple means.

EXAMPLE 11

Levid has a spiky, angular tune and attracts mocking comments from his listeners:

LEVID: You've not heard about Charlie the great
　　　　　And all his latest hits?
(Vs. 1) You've not heard about Jenny his bird,
　　　　　Singer preferred above all?
ALL:　　　　　　　　　　　　　　　　No!
LEVID:　　　　　　　　　　　　　　That's absurd!
ALL:　　What a shame, what a shame,
　　　　　That there is so much in a name,
　　　　　What a downright shame!

The words and music to the choruses from the first and last scenes were now learnt. During the third, fourth and fifth sessions the children took part in movement exercises in the gymnasium in an attempt to loosen them up, both physically and imaginatively. A teacher of creative gymnastics ran these sessions. A small drum (tambour) was used to assist in the timing of some actions. Simple methods of exploring space around the body in quick, slow, direct and peripheral movements of arms, legs, head and the whole body took place. It was found that a few of the boys were inhibited at their first encounter with such an approach, but they soon warmed up and by the fifth and sixth week of rehearsals were quite involved in creating actual dances. Various recordings including pop and electronic music were used as a stimulation to imaginative sequences.

As mentioned previously, part of the concept of the opera was to involve the chorus in singing and dancing at the same time. The next step was to combine the two media – the songs they had learnt and the sequences they had improvised – into an organized whole. Because of exits, entries, curtains and lighting effects which were relevant to the theatrical 'projection' required, we were limited to a stage. However, it was fairly large and we were able to extend our action over the orchestra pit, into the audience. We included also two levels of platform (disguised school rostra) on the stage itself. This enabled us to bring all the dancers into view, and allowed the group playing on the rear platform to be seen. They had *no* difficulty in being heard!

The five songs in scenes 2, 3 and 4 were accompanied by an acoustic (non-electric) guitar offstage for two ballads, or by the three staff members on the production team, who played piano, bass and drums. Working on the same principle as in *Not with a Bang* the trio was situated at the side-front, thus allowing the singers direct contact, dramatically and musically, with their audience. These songs – a fast duet in 5/4 time, an ensemble involving odd bars of 7/8 and 9/8 plus a fiercely syncopated rhythm, and a

1920s music-hall number for the gnarled Wontie in his brief moment of exuberance – required players other than the main protagonists in the play (members of the group itself), for they were now involved in dialogue, and in a completely new setting (see Example 12, 'Once').

The greatest creative challenge came from the Hades scene. I had not written music for this, but simply given general outlines of the five episodes in the scene in order that the children might create their own music. This was to be tape-recorded as soon as possible so that the chorus could get together immediately on a dance drama, involving colourful costumes, half

EXAMPLE 12

masks and imaginative lighting. We began work by finding two tape-recorders, three small microphones and a fairly resonant room. We had three large loud-speakers which, during the final production, were set around the sides and back of the auditorium.

A group of about twelve boys and girls was selected to organize and produce the sounds for this drama within the drama. On a Saturday afternoon we listened to recordings of excerpts from Stockhausen's *Song of the Children*, The Pink Floyd (a pop group popular at the time) and the soundtrack of the film *Space Odyssey 2001*. For specifically vocal expression we listened to parts of Penderecki's *Saint Luke Passion*, thus acquainting the children with the enormous possibilities of expressive sound material available which is not necessarily bound by the diatonic or even the twelve-note system of musical composition. This was, of course, a loosening-up exercise for the imagination rather than a technical or analytical study. From here we went immediately into experimenting with sounds ourselves. The microphone itself, used in a variety of positions, can yield a wide range of different sounds. A vocal range from low bass G to high soprano and beyond also offers great possibilities, particularly in conjunction with the usual three-speed settings found on the average tape-recorder.

Having spent three or four hourly sessions on taping short sections of our efforts – even getting so far as to jot down patterns, graphs and symbols, which to us at least represented a notation of these sounds – a final tape was made and given to the movement director. The five sequences we followed were, roughly:

(1) entry of masked, underworld figures, cloaked and sinister – mainly boys;

(2) entry of the more colourful personifications of the several aspects of Hades – mainly girls; interaction and free dance;

(3) entry of a masked Levid and Jenny (not the real characters, but of similar build);

(4) Art's pleading for Jenny to be released from both Levid and Hades. His rejection by a mocking Levid and an indifferent Jenny;

(5) closing dance, figures encircling the retreating couple, and end of scene.

A detailed lighting plot had to be prepared for the senior boy who managed the standard switchboard. Costumes for the first and last scenes were easily arranged, being normal dress for teenagers on a night out. For the Hades scene both boys and girls made some of their costumes, the designing of which I left to two or three girls who suggested ideas. We also drew upon the standard wardrobe equipment of both schools for such items as cloaks, masks, tights and other useful materials. The final four weeks were spent in frantic activity involving extra rehearsals, scenery building (the children submitted designs) and in perfecting the drama and dance on stage.

Apart from the spontaneous participation of both the children and staff involved in the production, I must express my admiration for the heads of both schools in allowing – in fact encouraging – this type of work to be a part of the life of the children for whom they are responsible. From my own point of view it was an exciting and most satisfying project.

A musical play

W. A. N. WELBURN and ERIC A. BRYCE

In order to create and produce a large-scale work involving a group of secondary schools – not all from the same area – four teacher-qualities are required: enthusiasm, co-operation, skill and stamina. The aim in this instance is to illustrate one way of going about organizing a form of group activity which is becoming increasingly popular in schools where time, facilities and enlightened staff attitudes prevail.

Literature, history, legend and pure fantasy are all considered suitable source material upon which to build a 'plot' and instrumental music, choral and solo singing, dance and design are all geared to the needs and abilities of the child keen to be involved. The accent is unashamedly upon enjoyment rather than upon cathartic dramatic experience, and therefore there is a tendency to underplay scenes of intense drama and to emphasize beauty of sound, movement and design – both in costumes and sets. The dramatic experience is consequently able to assume a variety of forms.

W. A. N. Welburn read economics at London University, and is now headmaster of Seaton Boys' Technical High School, South Australia.

Eric Bryce gained practical experience in the world of commercial jazz, before graduating in music at Adelaide University. He is music adviser for the technical high schools in South Australia.

THE WORDS (W.A.N.W.)

The happy collaboration with my present colleague began as the result of our witnessing a school concert presented by a boys' secondary school, in which a series of very sketchy, unartistic and educationally doubtful 'turns' were presented to a captive audience. The presentation might have passed muster as an end-of-term school review for the brief beguiling of uncritical pupils, but the prestige of the school was endangered by this public performance. Moreover, it was obvious that there was much good talent among the performers. If only that talent were properly channelled and inspired!

On the school staff at that time were not only my music teacher colleague and myself but also an indefatigable and inspiring English teacher who had a great interest in stage production. It was not long before the three of us decided to attempt a musical play.

From the beginning the 'team' went from strength to strength. Two of our musical plays have been performed by boys and girls representing over twenty-five secondary schools in successive arts festivals in Adelaide. The project thus expanded from the original linking of two neighbourhood boys' and girls' schools to an enterprise involving staff from many schools, annual music-drama camps and, indeed, the prestige of the State's technical high schools – which correspond closely to the British secondary modern schools.

THE LIBRETTO

The writing of a libretto for a musical play is not difficult for the teacher who has some imagination, a liking for rhyme and rhythm and some experience in the school-drama field. No technical knowledge of music is needed beyond the ability to hum – or whistle – a variety of well-known tunes. The librettist's most important requirement is a knowledge and understanding of the boys and girls to be concerned in the play, their abilities, limitations, potentials and interests. The fact that the writing of a full script with lyrics is time-consuming will not deter the enthusiast from what is a most satisfying and rewarding project.

Generally speaking, the basic plot should be gay and happy. The satisfaction of having taken part in a colourful and melodious presentation exceeds the pupil's expectations. Daring, swashbuckling heroes, lovely heroines awaiting rescue from danger, clear-cut, unpleasant villains and comic types with smart repartee, are all perennial favourites. Include with these a collection of subsidiary but essential short parts, walkers-on, crowd-fillers, slave-girls, soldiers, townsfolk – whatever is appropriate to the theme – and you have a ready-made large cast prepared to bring your imagination to life on stage.

For the beginner, adaptations of folk legends such as *Aladdin, Cinderella,* or *Jack and the Beanstalk*, or favourite stories from well-known literature such as *Tom Sawyer, Treasure Island, Little Women,* offer interesting possibilities; the plots are freely available and adaptations of several scenes in a sequence involving one or two acts is made relatively easy. Once the mind is allowed to roam freely among the myriad possibilities of themes and characters, a basic plot will emerge upon which the play can be built.

Avoid long speeches and keep the story moving; allow as many characters as possible to have a say in the development of the tale; avoid the temptation to moralize, philosophize or ride a hobby-horse; allow the simple clear dialogue and sequence of events to recount the story. Many of the songs will suggest themselves through the nature of the characters or in the development of the story. An opening chorus is most desirable, either immediately on 'curtain up' or after a brief prologue. This chorus could be given a reprise somewhere in the play, perhaps at the end of the first act (assuming that a two-act work is under construction) or to round off the whole show before the final curtain. A second chorus could open act 2 and be used again somewhere within the act – perhaps as theme music for a dance drama or ballet.

The hero and heroine suggest a duet; the villain and his henchmen a trio or quartet. The 'Father' character, whether he be mayor, admiral, chieftain or emperor, will have a song preferably with chorus. Solos will suggest themselves for other main parts. In a two-act musical play ten to twelve musical items should be included, but this does not necessarily imply the composition of ten or twelve different songs. In three or four cases, reprises or variations of the original melody may be used to advantage. For an hour's performance – one act – in three or four scenes, four or five compositions may be all that is necessary.

The purpose of the lyric in the play is to suggest the nature of the song or chorus. The opening chorus should indicate where we are, what we are doing there, what mood we are in and even what we might expect to happen. The introduction of chief characters is often an added purpose. A gay opening to the play demands a rhythmic and melodious chorus which may well become the theme-song of the play itself. Songs may anticipate or consolidate a position, or consider what has passed; they may comment on a situation or character; they often (particularly in the case of choruses) intensify or dramatize more fully the words and actions of a character. The appearance of a song should, of course, not be haphazard but clearly anticipated.

Fantasy in dance-drama and ballet offers many possibilities to the imaginative writer and choreographer, as do dream sequences and soliloquies. The hero, in a dilemma, can see the alternative courses of action danced before him. The evil thought of the villain may come to life in dance drama and the aspirations of the heroine can be presented in ballet form.

It may be objected that children at some schools have little or no talent for this kind of musical play. In our experience this is far from the truth, provided that the dialogue and lyrics are clear and meaningful. Some of the best performers come from the 'lower' streams, from pupils who have never before performed in public, and even from school 'misfits' whose behaviour and emotional problems have retarded their academic progress. Their participation in such a project has often brought new or revised motives into their lives which hitherto had little or no purpose. The sympathy and intelligent understanding, coaxing and cheerful discipline of the producer must be apparent. Even a skilful and reasonably experienced teacher will find this role intensely wearying, but satisfying beyond his pedagogic dreams.

In girls' or co-educational schools there is usually a nucleus of ballet dancers, girls who attend elementary dance or ballet classes, and who delight in showing audiences their art. Boys are more difficult to coax into the dance, but if the dance is masculine in approach (a Cossack dance, for instance), or if there has been a systematic approach to modern dance drama through a series of 'uninhibiting' sessions with a teacher familiar with the Laban–Slade methods there is usually little problem here.

The script–music link is a vital one, and there must be sympathetic collaboration between librettist and composer. Assuming that the librettist has considered his basic plot he will discuss the general features of the play with the composer; he will thus be aware of the 'flavour' of the music he is to write – Latin-American, modern, European, oriental, romantic, tragic and so on. If the story is set in Spain, the flavour will be Spanish, although not necessarily entirely so. There is always room for variety. In a recent successful production of such a play, while there were many 'Spanish' songs and choruses there was also an English music-hall patter song, and a delightfully clever song in the modern idiom.

Having agreed upon the general plot, author and composer may now think in terms of the basic idiom and further developments will soon manifest themselves. Now, from the staging point of view, the writer will consider the number of acts, scenes, main characters and subsidiaries, bearing in mind the running time of the play, the number of participants, the area of the school stage and possible financial restrictions. Lavish, spectacular productions are not a prerequisite of success.

The writing of the play follows, scene by scene, act by act. The writer must try to visualize his players against the appropriate backgrounds on a stage, acting their parts, moving and gesticulating, dressed in apt costume and wearing make-up, playing out their parts in a lighted arena. An aural imagination, as well as a visual one, is particularly important in order that audience reaction and sense of participation may be taken into account. There must be a variety in speech and character, clarity of ideas put into actors' mouths, and an easy sequence of events, dramatic points and climaxes.

At this stage the author need not worry unduly about lyrics, but he ought to have an idea as to the kind of song he wants at particular places. When the play is written, further collaboration with the composer is necessary. The librettist should then indicate the number, types and varieties of lyrics he proposes to include, and may point out suitable positions for dances. Assuming agreement upon these points, the author then proceeds to compose the lyrics. He will know what the songs' aims are, and, chiefly by trial and error, will produce a first attempt. The use of rhyme dictionaries, lexicons of synonyms and antonyms, a thesaurus and other aids are of value to the lyricist. If he examines the lyrics of popular songs, Gilbert and Sullivan ballads and choruses, musical comedy 'numbers' and the like, he will find considerable help in his initial attempts. Moreover, his composer colleague can offer at this stage practical assistance in rhythmical forms.

If the reader senses a vagueness of approach, a 'muddle-through' campaign, he is mistaken. In practice the collaboration produces exactly what the librettist and composer are seeking. Any differences which emerge at the frequent meetings of the two people concerned are *not* matters of principle (these were ironed out long before the dramatic writing was begun), but are usually matters of fitting together word–music phrases so that a smooth and attractive song emerges. W. S. Gilbert was reported to have stressed 'In the beginning, the word'. But in such enterprises as are envisaged here, no such edict or presumption should be allowed to dictate the relationship between lyricist and composer. The old give-and-take principle is of the utmost importance.

I cannot read a note of music and have very little idea of what goes on in a composer's mind, so I hand him my lyrics, tell him where the song occurs, who sings it, suggest the mood of the song, and maybe even go so far as to hum or whistle a tune which I have made up in my mind to fit the lyrics. Then I leave the composition entirely to him. At a later date I hear how he has fitted my words into his music, and, after some years of collaboration, I still find the experience intensely exciting and stimulating.

The English teacher on the staff is usually the one who finds himself involved in drama in school, and will no doubt be the popular choice for librettist and lyricist. He may not be the only teacher with imagination, but his close concern with language and literature, the techniques of composition of many kinds and his involvement with classroom dramatic activities fit him well for the position. He will not find himself a one-man band as help will come from many quarters. It is invariably the case that once some imaginative and energetic worker takes the plunge and provides the initial stimulus, his own enthusiasm and energy will attract others to his cause. His concern for the spoken word in his everyday duties is an added qualification, for he will gauge with accuracy the standard of dialogue to include in his play. His professional principles will almost automatically suggest a standard just above the 'norm'. This is desirable, for quality of performance is something which must be worked up to gradually.

The English teacher's contact with a variety of classes in the school provides a first means of inspiring pupil participation. A meeting of all those interested in assisting will almost certainly reveal a working number, and the assistance of other teachers to publicize and stimulate is most desirable. Many pupils volunteer to undertake 'offstage' duties; these boys and girls should certainly attend the initial meeting, for some of them will change their minds and volunteer for onstage work! Drama teachers know their class well from the point of view of acting abilities, and should be prepared to do much pressing and prompting to ensure the inclusion of known good actors. The 'unknowns' and 'untrieds' must have attention – often their talent is surprising. The class 'clown' almost invariably turns up for the initial meeting, eager to secure a comedy role. The class disrupter may well attend for purposes of exhibitionism; there is no better place for him than the disciplined atmosphere of the stage.

Many boys and girls will demur at first on the grounds that they cannot sing – especially when they find that chorus work is involved. But, since the composer is already aware of their limitations and has made due allowance in his compositions, fears of inability to succeed are quickly dispelled. Singing with others is not as difficult as solo work. Soloists will be revealed either by personal knowledge on the part of the music teacher, or by auditioning. The boy with the breaking voice, or the girl who is tone-deaf should not have their interest thwarted; the librettist will have allowed a small number of speaking parts in the play for just these people.

It is an excellent idea at the first meeting of interested boys and girls for the composer to play over one or two of the songs, and for the librettist to give a résumé of the play's content. The producer may at this point be able to say something of the proposed action, decor and costuming. The choreographer (not necessarily experienced, but a teacher who has some regard for the artistry and skill of mime and dance) should also speak of the part to be taken by dance in the play. It is vital to have the co-operation of teacher colleagues; their assistance will become ever more necessary as production time draws near, and their various skills and talents – as electricians, wardrobe mistresses, effects staff, stage managers, make-up artists, programme designers, publicity agents and workshop men – are brought more into the picture.

From here on, regular meetings should be the standard. A routine of rehearsals established early will become a habit to participants. Whether rehearsals are held in or out of school hours will depend upon school policy, but we have never found a lack of understanding or tolerance on the part of headmasters and others, who recognize in the project an educational endeavour whose value is often prized beyond the attainment of a certificate. At the same time, in over twenty years' experience in the field of musical plays, I have not found one instance of a performer who has suffered academically because of his involvement in such a school production. What is quite certain is that every performer, on- or offstage, increases in stature and well-being, gains self-confidence and finds an outlet for often woefully suppressed talent and self-expression. Many years after leaving school, the participants in such productions recall vividly their parts, the camaraderie, the tenseness and delight of public performance, with a vividness and enthusiasm never equalled in their recollection of routine, pedantic studies and school or public examinations!

Parents should be brought into the picture at an early stage. Rehearsal times and other appropriate information should be given to them. A number of parents may offer useful assistance although practical involvement of parents should be controlled – pupils are more at ease in rehearsals in the absence of parental witnesses.

The uninitiated, the doubters – and even the cynics – on the school staff will no doubt pose questions and problems. But once the show is on its way, even the most dubious will see some educational value in the production and by the time public performance is due, there will be little doubt in most minds of the value of the project.

THE MUSIC (E.A.B.)

Secondary school music drama must be able to capture youthful enthusiasm and consequently productions must be imbued with a spirit of life, colour, vigour and action. All these qualities are more readily attainable when the show is built around the talent available.

I was happy that my colleague decided to adapt scenes from the novel *Tom Sawyer* into a sequential musical play as our second combined venture. The success of my part as composer, arranger and musical director would depend on how well I could utilize the available musical talent.

From a total of 700 pupils in the school, there were 20 boys learning instruments privately. Of these instrumentalists, only a guitarist, bassist, drummer and one accordion player had received more than two years' tuition, possessed an inbuilt musicianship and could be relied upon to play in a tuneful and musical manner. It was obvious that the orchestral score had to be moulded around them. These factors helped to decide what form our production would take, and led to the decision that the musical atmosphere needed for *Tom Sawyer* would be enhanced by a well-played piano accordion. In the real sense of theatre, a solo piano accompaniment would have killed our production, and above all I was determined to avoid the rut that the majority of school productions had fallen into – Gilbert and Sullivan, with the principal parts sung and acted by ex-pupils, the orchestral score played on a piano by a teacher or paid accompanist, and the bulk of pupils standing as props singing the choruses in one or two parts.

Before planning the instrumental side of the score, much consideration would have to be given to the available singing and acting talent before tunes and keys could be selected. Owing to the life that our producer was able to inject into these projects, we had literally hundreds of applicants for auditions. A good deal of the incentive arose from the fact that it was a matter of tradition to combine with the neighbourhood girls' school.

There were, however, no trained voices among the pupils and the same old problem recurred – some that had a flair for acting were unable to sing in tune, and others with true voices lacked any acting ability. Here again, the choice of our production proved sound. Short, ballad-type tunes for the principals, and rousing single chorus lines, with an occasional venture into parts of alternate melodic phrases and descants, were required.

'TOM SAWYER'
The opening bars of the main chorus are an excellent starting point for some analysis of the music, both vocal and instrumental. Before detailing this, however, it is important to remember that the tune was written bearing in mind the two following factors: the time of preparation for production was limited to three months, and all rehearsals had to take place outside normal school hours. The initial stages of rehearsal were a one-hourly session per week for chorus work; and approximately thirty boys and thirty girls with ages ranging from thirteen to seventeen years had qualified for chorus roles. As stated before, none of these pupils had trained voices, could sight-sing or possessed any developed musical facility. There was no real definition of the voices into categories. Despite these deficiencies a natural tunefulness coupled with unbounded enthusiasm was evident.

With these considerations dictating the course of melodic flow, I began work on the opening chorus.

There would have to be a melodic range that would allow all pupils to fall naturally into two main voice types – high and low – and at the same time permit them to sing the complete melody with a minimum of strain (see Example 1). Simple chorus-verse style lyrics demanded a catchy tune that

EXAMPLE I

would enable pupils to learn and retain with a minimum of repetition. Therefore, except for the addition of occasional 'natural feel' descant phrases which

EXAMPLE 2

would give a quality of vocal depth, the chorus would consist of a single-line melody. This would allow the singers to concentrate on tone, clarity and volume, while engaging in the necessary stage movements that are so vital to live performances.

Looking at the vocal line in Example 2 – 'Mighty river' – a forthright, syncopated but simple melodic statement, built on the tonic chord, is answered by a more plaintive phrase which is harmonized by chords that suggest modal qualities. The majority of the cast sang this melodic line (either as written or an octave lower) and a selected group sang the split descant phrases.

The community-styled phrases of bars 1–4 reflect the happy-go-lucky rollicking life on the river, while the answering phrases of bars 5–8 conjure up qualities which reflect the age and spirit of the river. Answering phrases such as these with their accompanying modal sounds helped to keep the tune from becoming trite.

The instrumental score was designed to allow the previously-mentioned, small group of musicians to function effectively with a minimum of rehearsal and practice time. Limited instrumental standard of the pupils, both in their inability to read quickly and surely and their lack of polished performing technique, created the situation where instrumental arrangements, if cluttered with notes and technical detail, would impose an immediate restriction, and render their playing lifeless and ineffective.

I found the arranging techniques of the commercial and jazz musicians invaluable in sketch-scoring for inexperienced instrumentalists of school age. Of these techniques, the most important is the use of the *chord symbol*, the value of which music educationists are at long last realizing.

A chord symbol is a letter that stands for a certain chord, for example, C is the symbol for the chord of C major and it automatically implies that the notes C E G can be played. Therefore when a rhythm guitarist, pianist, piano accordion player or bassist is confronted with the symbol C written above the melody line, his natural musicality allows him to play the notes of the chord with a minimum of reading effort, in whatever style is demanded. Some other chord symbols with their corresponding chord notes are shown in Example 3. The need in *Tom Sawyer* was for a strong, fundamental,

EXAMPLE 3

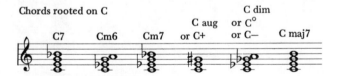

rhythmic and harmonic accompaniment and the instruments at hand were admirably suited to fill this requirement (see Example 4).

The piano accordion provided a strong melody in the right hand, while the left hand supplied the polka-like, octave-chord bass. Note the shorthand method of Example 4. No bass line is necessary for this instrument as the chord symbols tell the player what bass-buttons are to be used in the left hand.

EXAMPLE 4

The guitarist provided the off-beat harmonic accompaniment. A bar of the simple rhythm is written with the occasional change of chord symbols, which would be read from the piano accordion line, being the only other guide needed for instant performance.

The double bass–bass guitar has the fundamental root and fifth notes of each chord. This basic formula, so prevalent in folk songs, although boring in the sense of developed bass lines, is none the less harmonically true and effective. It also helps to develop a natural 'feel' for bass line progressions in the young musician.

Only two of the components of the complete modern drum kit are used here: the ride (sizzle) cymbal (16–24 inches diam.) and the side drum. This simple repetitive rhythm blends well with the sounds of the bass and guitar. No bass drum was required. The booming sound of the bass drum, even if played lightly, would spoil the harmonious, rhythmic and warm sounds of the guitar and bass.

The important character of Huckleberry Finn was played by a lad who, while possessing some acting ability, lacked singing talent. Therefore the personality of Huck had to be projected through declamatory monologues. With a simple, but mischievous and rather defiantly-spirited waif in mind, I based Huck's verse of the trio 'Just three lads' on the jazz form known as the 'blues'. This provided the necessary contrast between the 'pampered goodness' of Willie's verse and the good-natured but rather impish boyishness of Tom's verse.

The fundamental harmonic sequence of the twelve-bar blues is built on the major chords I, IV and V, with each having an added minor seventh; for example, in the key of C the notes of the chords are as shown in Example 5.

EXAMPLE 5

A fundamental 'blues' sequence is shown in Example 6.

EXAMPLE 6

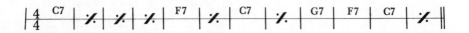

Three bars of Huck's verse, 'I'm a real bad boy', are shown in Example 7. Observe the boogie-woogie left-hand bass line; and the immediate rearrangement of the blues harmonic formula.

Example 8 shows two bars of the sketch arrangement that was in fact placed before the young musicians, who (after I had explained tempo, style and sequence) were able to play the music almost immediately with a minimum of errors. Notice the minor–major, common chord bass notes.

EXAMPLE 7

EXAMPLE 8

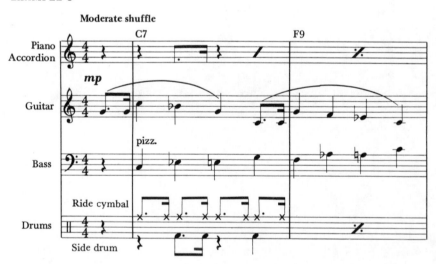

In Huck's solo, 'I ain't much good', the lyrics demanded a more sympathetic and slightly plaintive tune. Here was Huck in a more melancholy
mood and to help to create this effect the melody was harmonized with modal
inflections (see Example 9). Although the chords are rooted on I, IV and V

EXAMPLE 9

(in relation to the key note G) and the key signature suggests G minor, the varying use of B♭ and B♮; E♭ and E♮; F♯ and F♮ together with the final cadence of the chord built on F resolving to the G major chord, give the modal sound.

The instrumental accompaniment proved very effective and was similar in style to Example 8 with a slightly amplified but mellow guitar playing the melody and the other instruments providing a sympathetic background.

One of the joys of the 'home-grown' musical play is to observe the development of some of the hitherto musical nondescripts in the cast. Such was the case with the lad who played the part of Jim. As it happened he was the head prefect, a big lad, and to the delight of us all, he produced (with a little persuasion) a rough but rich and true bass–baritone voice. It was decided to write two songs expressly for him. The producer managed wonders with the cotton-field scene and Jim's singing lives vividly in my memory as one

EXAMPLE 10

of the richest musical moments I have experienced in my career as a music teacher.

The spiritual was written in a simple rubato style which allowed Jim to express his range and tone in a repeated short nine-bar verse: an extract is shown in Example 10. The chorus section of the spiritual, four bars of which are shown in Example 11, has the girls singing a descant based on a descending chromatic run, and the boys taking the melody proper. The harmonization of bar 4 in Example 10 – a rather odd sound (the minor chord built on the third degree of the scale) – is a more elemental 'horn' sound than the natural harmonization of the supertonic eleventh passing

EXAMPLE 11

EXAMPLE 12

to the dominant ninth illustrated in Example 12. The instrumental
accompaniment consisted of the guitar and bass playing in a basic block
harmonic style that was similar to the piano voicing of Examples 10 and 11.
In this case both lads read from a line of chord symbols (see Example 13).

EXAMPLE 13

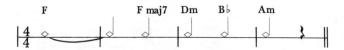

The guitarist slowly strummed the chords at the rate shown by the notes
of length and the bassist played the letter name of each chord symbol.

The sign 'segue' led straight to the fervent negro protest song 'River
calling'. This song contains lyrics that demand a mature singer to convey
the depth of meaning within. Jim rose to the occasion magnificently. The
first verse was sung in a free, rubato style and the second in a strict and very
fast 2/4. Because the theme of the play centres around the Mississippi I
decided that the opening chorus 'Mighty river' and 'River calling' should be
closely related in melodic and harmonic style in an effort to create a mood
link. The same key (B♭) was used primarily because it best suited the singer's
natural range. The style of the song together with the piano accompaniment
are illustrated in the few bars of Example 14.

There was another surprise in store for us in the form of a young lad who
had been studying ballet for a number of years. Not only was he well
disciplined in the classical and modern ballet but he also possessed a natural
flair for dance improvisation. In the girls' school we knew of a pupil who was
an experienced ballerina. Now, quite unexpectedly, we had found her a
partner.

EXAMPLE 14

Our producer drew the blueprint of the form of the ballet and as he was also the choreographer, I listened very carefully as he expressed his ideas, endeavouring at the same time to formulate a suitable musical sequence.

8

The 'Ballet macabre' as it was called, took place in the eerie and ghostly atmosphere of McDougal's cave. It unfolded its story in the unreal and grotesque world of dreams. I decided on four short but connected movements that had an overall performance time of approximately four minutes with a gradual increase in tempo and dynamics ending in a frenzied climax. Because of the conflicting elements of good and evil within the play I decided to use some of the vocal material already written, and rearrange it into a set of stylized, slightly burlesques motifs:

(1) 'The world of sleep' (see Example 15a). Bats stir as the atmosphere is set with veiled repeated bass notes, seventh chords and glissandos. The haunting melody of Huck's solo, 'I ain't much good', played in a more sustained and sombre style, ushers in the first of the evil spirits.

EXAMPLE 15a

(2) 'Life: delight!' (see Example 15b). The tempo quickens as the happy-go-lucky tune of Tom's 'Life's a big delight' is changed into a devilish mockery.

(3) 'Gabriel: devil' (see Example 15c). A basic, well-defined but crude rhythm introduces an equally toneless and debased version of Jim's spiritual. The forces of evil are prevailing. Compare Example 15c and Example 10, on p. 98.

EXAMPLE 15b

EXAMPLE 15c

(4) 'Injun Joe' (see Example 15d). A new bass motif accompanied by frenzied tremolos sees the spirit form of Injun Joe with a knife in hand in threatening poses. As Becky screams, Tom wakes and the apparitions vanish.

EXAMPLE 15d

To illustrate the extremes of difference possible in this type of musical play, I propose to describe briefly a second successful musical produced by the same two high schools the following year.

With the loss of many of our previous stars a new set of talent had to be sought. This group of pupils presented us with a different range of abilities that demanded an entirely fresh approach in order to be utilized suitably. The musical that emerged was an Eastern fastasy entitled *The Enchanted Garden*.

'THE ENCHANTED GARDEN'

The following three factors dictated the form and style of the writing of this musical:

(1) there were senior pupils in both boys' and girls' schools who had the experience and ability to take leading roles, both acting and singing, of a moderately developed nature;

(2) ballet and folk dancing were very active in the girls' school and there were boys who were willing to take part in masculine dances;

(3) the variety of the instrumentalists in the schools had increased, and their ability improved.

Of the long list of songs, dances and ballets written for this play I have chosen as examples those which, I hope, will help to demonstrate the scope and development of the music that the available pupil talent could perform successfully.

A rollicking and tuneful opening chorus was required, so in preference to writing parts that would have tested and probably hindered an untrained ear, a two-part melodic chorus was decided upon (see Example 16). In the first and third verses where the two melodies were used, the boys took the melody proper in a hearty, masculine style and the girls sang the counter-melody to the syllable *la* in a light-hearted and bright manner.

EXAMPLE 16

There are at least four principles that will aid in the development of a safe, tuneful and colourful instrumental sound:

(1) a thorough realization of each pupil's ability. This will ensure that the all-important melodic and counter-melodic lines will be well performed;

(2) a basic appreciation of each instrument's practical range when in the hands of inexperienced pupils. Such knowledge gained through experience will keep intonation problems to a minimum and enable the players to sustain their chordal notes and articulate their rhythmic figures in a tuneful and relaxed manner;

(3) a reasonable knowledge of harmony as applied to fundamental chord progressions will enable the production of full, strong and colourful textures, regardless of the size of the ensemble;

(4) the developed facility to think in different keys for the transposing of instruments will reduce errors and omission of accidentals.

The instrumental complement for the *Garden* consisted of: flute, descant recorder, two alto saxophones, three B♭ trumpets, two E♭ horns, guitar, bass, piano and percussion. The flute, guitar, bass, drummer and the first trumpet and saxophone players were all moderately good readers capable of playing in tune. This allowed more imaginative scoring. Example 17 shows a scored extract of the chorus theme which in this 3/4 form constitutes a section of the overture and makes up the 'enchanted' ballet. Notice how the melody changes hands every four bars (guitar, flute-recorder, saxophone) and that there is some connecting movement to tie up these melodic phrases. For example, the flute and the recorder in bars 3 and 4 lead naturally into their theme entry in bar 5, thus providing interest while the guitar sustains the note D. In bars 7 and 8 the trumpets provide the link by announcing the saxophone entry and also emphasize the implied modulation to the supertonic. The harmonic depth and waltz lilt are supplied by the 'old faithfuls' the bass (bowed) and the guitar. No drums were used as they would have tied down the rhythm and inhibited the freedom required for the tempo changes of some of the phrases.

EXAMPLE 17

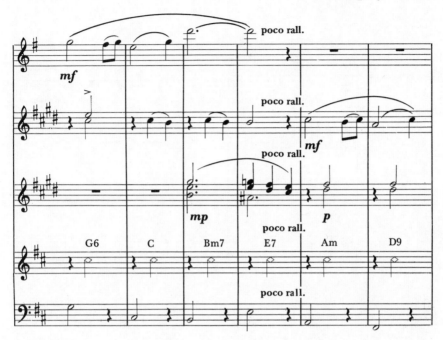

As the play was set in the mythical land of Syrabia, a Middle-Eastern motif was required. Naturally a 'pseudo' idiom had to be used to give the flavour of the fabulous East and in Hassan's solo a hint of such a style is obvious (see Example 18). This flattened supertonic idiom could be used

EXAMPLE 18

because of the singer's ability to sing difficult intervals with ease. It would have been pointless to set a lot of songs in this 'pseudo' style and the majority of the music was harmonized in a manner that best suited the mood required. Example 19 shows a section of the stylized score with the repeated 'drone' F bass notes and the flattened supertonic flute figures providing the nebulous harmonic background to a portion of Hassan's solo.

A musical highlight was the madrigal. The presence of five girls with very clear, true and well produced soprano voices, made the inclusion of such

EXAMPLE 19

a song possible. Added to this was the developed instrumental complement of flute, recorder, acoustic guitar and double bass. Because of its legitimate presentation this item needed a lot of concentrated rehearsal, but the intense work that went into its making was richly rewarded as its performance was enthusiastically received by the audience. Example 20 shows an extract of the rather intricate writing.

Visiting suitors from distant lands, who sought the hand of the princess, afforded the opportunity for the inclusion of three exotic dances. In the Siamese dance (see Example 21) the melodic interest was maintained by the flute and saxophone, while the bass, xylophone, cymbal and drums set a repeated rhythmic pattern that conjured up an oriental atmosphere.

EXAMPLE 20

A love duet in the true sense of operetta was included. An extract of the chorus of this song 'If dreams came true' is shown in Example 22 and illustrates the melodic and harmonic style. Habiba handled her part well, but Kassim was unable to inject into his part the necessary lyrical, sensitive and mature qualities needed to make the duet the success we had hoped it would be.

EXAMPLE 21

The final chorus was a little more adventurous in melodic style with canonic type entrances, and a definite voicing of parts as illustrated in Example 23. To create the required grandiose effect, broad and constantly moving harmonies add the depth and colour in the lower registers.

It is to be hoped that this brief description of the two completely different types of musicals used as examples will be of some value to teachers contemplating a similar involvement, particularly in regard to the importance of taking into account the available pupils, background and abilities. To

EXAMPLE 22

a teacher, the satisfaction of seeing the enthusiastic efforts of the pupils bearing fruit in the form of successful performances, and the obvious development of character and ability, is richly rewarding.

As a musician with an urge to write, I find that the field of school music offers itself as a testing ground for ideas and as an opportunity for the performance of original works, which, in some cases, because of their diatonic and lyrical qualities may be classed as 'old hat' in the world of the experimentalist, and therefore not worthy of performance.

EXAMPLE 23

From improvisation into drama

DEREK WEEKS

The following two reports of school plays prepared entirely through the creative powers of older children working together with two or three able and enthusiastic teachers are indicative of the kind of similar work being done in various schools in the United Kingdom. As if to confound the reactionary producer who has little time for such 'vague wanderings', Derek Weeks makes it quite clear that the unity of dramatic expression is maintained – by placing acting, music, movement and design on level terms with each other – and that his teaching methods and his desire that the children help themselves through self-expression and critical analysis of the work in hand are constantly in his mind.

Such a teacher has obviously taken trouble to acquire the latest ideas and techniques in the fields of child drama, the use of the new music in education, and has a working knowledge of and interest in the theatre, both traditional and contemporary. At the centre of his vital approach to education is the child, not the drama. Yet it is becoming clearer in the areas of educational research that both child and drama are inextricably interwoven, and in this respect Derek Weeks is inviting us to view some of the possibilities in a dramatic approach to society and to history. However, it must be borne in mind that the aim here is to produce a complete play, a finished product, and not simply to act out an exciting episode from a history book. In pedantic hands the process of re-enacting scenes from the past – or present – is going to hinder rather than help the child to be aware of himself and the world in which he lives and moves. The essence of his approach lies in encouraging and stimulating a dramatic view of all aspects of life. In his own words:

'The play changed the lives of many of the children concerned. For the first time they became absorbed in something they could do well ... For the first time, too, the audience, few of whom were patrons of the theatre, realized that it can be entertaining when instructive ... It was a most exciting project to work on, and because it was original it provided a new concept for the school play.'

Derek Weeks, formerly head of drama and a senior house master at Lawrence Weston School, Bristol, is now a lecturer in speech and drama at the College of St Matthias, Bristol. A member of the Schools' Council Drama Panel, he was also a founder-member of the Bristol Arts Centre, where he has directed plays by Arden, Durenmatt, Kopit, Livings, Orton, Wilde, and Wood.

'JOHN'S BROWN BODY'

The play *John's Brown Body* developed from a course in drama and art held on Thursday afternoons in 1965–6 as part of a sixth-form recreational session; the alternatives offered included ice-skating, horse-riding, and judo. Our aim was to try to explore some of the affinities between drama and art and to try to use the stage to synthetize them. Ten pupils chose to work on the course, three boys and seven girls, together with the art teacher and myself.

The boys were known to be lively, relatively uninhibited and verbally fluent. The girls were more of an unknown quantity but appeared at first to be quiet and reserved. Unlike the boys, the girls had had no theatrical experience, and no one in the group had done drama as a subject before. Bearing all this in mind we decided that it would be better to start with speech rather than movement. In any case we knew that the boys could talk and so we decided to make them lead the others.

The first talking point was a painting by Chagall, an odd picture, full of colour, strange shapes and faces. We began by asking the group to describe the painting generally and went on to discuss the characters, attempting to establish them as individuals and then relating them to the others. The conversation became increasingly interesting and even the quiet girls became absorbed and made contributions. Ideas began to flow freely, and eventually we improvised a story suggested by the group about an artist and his relationship with his friends, models and his work. The result was interesting. Everyone in the group took part, joining in the improvisation when they felt they could add something to its development. This made a lively play which had some depth and provided us with a lot more to talk about.

It was most important, in an extended course of this kind, that the first session should go well. Everyone worked for as much of the time as possible, and everyone's ideas were tried, good or bad. In this way the qualities of concentration and absorption were increased and the pupils gained in confidence. In fact, one of the boys became so interested in this first idea that he borrowed the picture and wrote a play based on it which he later produced.

We next decided to explore the artist's problems in creating his work. We talked about art in everyday objects, arguing a great deal about Warhol's 'Tide' boxes and films, and *objets d'art* like Picasso's *Venus du Gaz*. In the hall where we worked were large piles of stacking chairs; the group made them into shapes. The structures ranged from a literal conveyor belt to a matador and bull, and abstractions such as Heaven and Hell. After making them we left them and went outside to look for interesting objects in and around an old ruined building in the school grounds. All sorts, shapes and sizes were found – bricks, a rusty sewing-machine, pulleys, springs and general scrap. The pupils brought them back and were asked to make them into 'sculptures'. Set against the chair structures these formed a strange surrealist world. We asked the group how what had been created could be used in a dramatic context. They suggested that the setting could be the aftermath of a nuclear attack and that they could take on the character of the objects they had found. Conversations were started, enlarged and deepened between such characters as an eye, a boot, a sewing-machine and a matador's cloak. This became an amusing and often poignant comment on the human condition and, on reflection, this was one of the few sessions where we really found a connection between the creative processes in art and drama.

For the third session we decided to base the work on the framework of an apparently simple story, and suggest deeper meanings involving symbolism and allegory. We took Jonah and the whale as our basis, read the story and asked for ideas. One girl suggested that we write a song about Jonah and use it as a narrative device. The whole group tried this and we ended up with six ballads and tunes to work from. Gradually a story was evolved and the modern parallel of the spy emerged. This became a rather sinister work, tense and sometimes tongue-in-cheek but although it bore some resemblance to the original, rarely reached the standard of our previous work.

However, the group's obvious enjoyment of the work we had been doing and their growing awareness of a variety of unexpected talents being shown, suggested that we might work towards something more ambitious and tangible. Having seen Joan Littlewood's production of *Oh ! What a Lovely War* and having been concerned in the opening Bristol Arts Centre production of *Hang Down your Head and Die* I had become very interested in this form of theatre. Some of the sixth-form students had seen the dress rehearsal of *Hang Down your Head and Die* and had been impressed both by its theatrical impact and the thoughts it provoked. The Arts Centre had made a tape of their production and we borrowed this together with the scripts. We spent the fifth session reading and listening to the play (the fourth was spent watching a matinee performance of *The Merchant of Venice* at the Theatre Royal). The pupils were greatly taken with the style and effect of the work and immediately suggested what we had hoped – that we should take a similar topic, find out as much about it as we could and present it as the school play. This would be the ideal opportunity to use the stage as we had originally hoped. We asked them to think the suggestion over carefully before the next session and to be ready to suggest a possible subject – preferably controversial and of contemporary relevance.

We approached the sixth afternoon somewhat apprehensively, but the colour problem was suggested as a possible theme. This was welcomed unanimously as being of crucial importance to all of us and, besides, no one else at that time had tackled it on stage in the way we intended. The rest of the session was taken up with a discussion of ways and means of approaching the subject, possible methods of presentation and sources of material. The historical problems of slavery, immigration, and the American scene were discussed, and the brilliant idea of presenting the play as a sort of Black and White Minstrel Show with a live band came from one of the boys. The pupils were so enthusiastic about the idea that we decided to collect as much information as possible between us by the following week and work from there.

From this moment the sessions rarely became defined. They were spent in culling factual information from a wide variety of books, national and local newspapers, and colour supplements. We worked individually, in small groups, and occasionally as a complete group. Sometimes we would spend an hour garrulously improvising only to discover that a simpler, better idea took five minutes. Gradually, in this way, the good ideas were retained and the bad ones discarded; talking merely for the sake of talking was jumped on by all concerned, and the improvisations became tighter and more polished as confidence grew. As we became more expert in linking techniques to information obtained, our material began to increase in variety and volume until we reached the stage where careful moulding into a structured outline was needed.

To find this we returned to the two plays already mentioned. Both start with a song-and-dance routine. We decided to do the same. First we enlisted the help of a member of the mathematics department, who was a former professional musician. To him fell the task of arranging, often at very short notice, all the music and getting together a sixteen-piece band. This consisted of his own school jazz band supplemented by four or five professional musicians. The resulting 'sound' contributed greatly to the impact of the production. After much argument and experiment we eventually chose four Negro-type songs and wrote different words for them:

> Our slave master's coming today
> Doo-dah, doo-dah
> Give us a whipping instead of pay
> Doo-dah, doo-dah-day.

and:

> Ha ha hah, you and me
> Little black man we don't like thee.

Many hours were spent working out the dance routines as they built up to a climax where our theme was stated – the ridiculous domination of coloured people by whites – by the movement of the chorus around a coloured solo singer, and his eventual engulfment by the majority.

The play was designed in two acts. The first outlined some events of the history of slavery, giving many facts and using theatrical techniques to emphasize them. The second act explored the colour problem now. As the play was conceived as a show we decided to link the scenes by using a compère. He had to link all the long sequences we had worked out and generally keep the play moving. Following the song-and-dance routine the compère led straight into an African village sequence set to music in a calypso rhythm – originally composed for Jonah and the whale. The villagers danced and sang:

> We are happy in our own land
> Far away from any master's hand
> We are happy to be by ourselves ...

Sailors entered and took them to their ship. As the set consisted of black rostra and ropes only it was relatively easy to change scenes quickly by lighting, so the stage immediately became the ship's deck. Slides were flashed on the cyclorama giving details of slave ships, their crews, conditions, sizes, speeds, whilst two narrators underlined many of the facts:

1ST MAN: Most ships lasted only about ten voyages.
2ND MAN: About half the Liverpool ships had girls' names.

(*The band plays 'Sweet Sue' and snatches of other tunes containing girls' names. Two girls in bikinis walk on the stage carrying boxes two feet high. They stand on them as though winners of a beauty contest.*)

1ST MAN: The slave decks below were usually about two feet high.

(*The crew drive the slaves into the area provided by the boxes, the girls run off horrified.*)

2ND MAN: At night, in bad weather, during epidemics, and whenever there was fear of mutiny, the slaves were kept in these kennels chained together.
1ST MAN: Let us not, however, forget the humanity of the captains. Men and women were stowed separately, children usually with the women, and the women usually not chained.
SLAVE: The consequences of this overcrowding were of course disease and death.
2ND MAN: A Spanish priest in 1582 said:
PRIEST: The very stench is enough to kill most of them.

This section continued in this vein ending with:

2ND MAN: Of both Bristol and Liverpool, then the second and third biggest cities of England, it was at various times said ...
BOTH: There is not a brick in the city which is not cemented by the blood of a slave.

9

It was followed by a quick guide to Bristol. Slides of familiar Bristol scenes were projected and a guide told a party of tourists all about their associations with the slave trade, leading into a slave auction sung to the tune of 'Coconuts' – 'I've got a loverly bunch of slaves up here'. After this came more facts:

1ST MAN: The Quakers said:
QUAKER: The slaves branded 'Society' by their owners, The Society for the Propagation of the Gospel, should be set free.
2ND MAN: It is time we formed an abolitionist society.
1ST MAN: Charles Wesley said:
WESLEY: Slaves, like whites, are children of God.

(*They all form a congregation and sing the Abolitionist hymn:*)

> We ask not that the slaves should lie
> As lies his master, at his ease,
> Beneath a silken canopy,
> Or in the shade of blooming trees.

(*This continues until a character dressed as Lord Nelson enters and says:*)

NELSON: I was bred in the good old school and taught to appreciate the value of our West Indian possessions, nor shall their interests be infringed while I have an arm to fight in their defence against the damnable and cursed doctrines of Wilberforce.

It was the cue for an outline of Wilberforce's life from his schooldays, through his struggle in Parliament to his ultimate victory in the vote to abolish slavery. For the final scene in Parliament we used the words of the main characters present. Pitt, for example, said:

> 'The dawn rides up with fiery steeds
> And brings us morning light
> But Afric's shore meanwhile grows dark
> Whose stars lead on the night.'

So says the poet Virgil. On us in England, the light of civilization sheds its beams. If we listen to the voice of reason and duty, we may hope that even Africa, though last of all the quarters of the globe, shall enjoy at length, in the evening of her days, those blessings that have descended so plentifully upon us. It is an atonement for our long and cruel injustice towards Africa that I shall vote for the measure proposed by my honourable friend.

The compère then changed the scene to America. The first half of the play ended with a long choral verse sequence taken from 'John Brown's Body' by Stephen Vincent Benet. The actions were played out on stage as the words were spoken and Brown was hanged. The band played softly throughout and the act ended with a pianissimo chord whilst the cast whispered:

Nothing is changed, John Brown, nothing is changed John . . . Brown.

Act 2 started with the same tableau and the same words, but the band played in a major key, and we were swiftly away with a sequence about modern America, referring to key Negro personalities, particularly James Meredith. After this five girls danced in with a large coloured ball which they threw slowly to each other, smiling emptily as the band played 'Falling in love with love', and talking gaily to the audience about many white American atrocities:

3RD GIRL: in the 16th Street Baptist Church in Birmingham, Alabama, a children's Bible class was being held. A lesson on 'The Love that forgives' had just ended. Suddenly a bomb hit the church exploding huge holes in the walls and killing 4 girls, 3 aged 14 and the other aged 11; 14 other Negroes were injured.

The compère then linked social attitudes towards coloured people and slaves in Ancient Greece and Rome with Shylock's feelings about being a Jew, and the Nazi Party Manifesto:

3RD NAZI: We demand that the State shall make it its first duty to promote the industry and livelihood of the citizens of the State. If it is not possible to nourish the entire population of the State, foreign nationals must be excluded from the Reich.

This was followed by two Englishmen in bowler hats and carrying umbrellas saying the same things as the Nazis but in words taken from statements by Conservative and Labour Members of Parliament.

1ST ENGLISHMAN: Immigration into this country should be limited to persons of sound health who have jobs and living accommodation arranged before they enter. Preference should be given to people holding British passports and immigrants should not be permitted to remain here without working, nor to overcrowd their housing accommodation.
2ND ENGLISHMAN: This is a British country with British standards of behaviour. The British must come first.

They were succeeded by a vindictive soap-box orator who showed the lop-sided attitude of many people in the community:

There are two points in this world that we all hate – Racial Segregation and coloured people. On buses we have to have blacks giving out our change – never smiling, not like our white conductors . . .

Then came the variety show act. Two characters came on, did a song and dance, ad libbed with the audience, and finally sang an audience participation song. For much of this scene the actors included every joke they could think of about 'wogs'. They actually sang a song called 'Wogs' to the tune 'Kids' from the popular musical *Oliver*.

Wogs! What's the matter with Wogs today?
Wogs! Who can understand anything they say?
Wogs! They think they own the whole ruddy world.
Black ones, brown ones, red and white striped ones,
And what about the workers?
Wogs! Name me one who can sing and dance.

(*A back projection of Sammy Davis Jr, Duke Ellington, Louis Armstrong, and Ella Fitzgerald.*)

Wogs! Name me one who is good at sport.

(*A back projection of Cassius Clay, Ralph Boston, the Harlem Globetrotters, and Jesse Owens.*)

Why can't they be like whites are
Perfect in every way,
Oh! What's the matter with Wogs today?

The audience participation song used the tune of 'Old MacDonald':

Old MacDonald had some slums, ee ay ee ay o.
And in these slums there were some blacks, ee ay ee ay o.
With a broken window here, leaky pipe there,
Here a hole, there a crack,
Everywhere a squeaky board.

Finally we showed the dilemma of the coloured immigrant looking for a flat and a job. The situations were taken from newspaper cuttings about West Indians, Indians and Africans, but ours became a Pakistani as the accent was easier. He was interviewed by a welfare officer, the manager of a large store, and six landladies and was rejected by all but one:

6TH LANDLADY: Oh! Certainly, I've got a lovely little room, lovely it is. Beautiful bed and a lovely room. Best room in the house you know. You can have it if you like. 'Course you'll have to share it with 23 other people. 'Ope you don't mind.

He was left alone while the loudspeakers played a recording we had made of people's comments in the local shopping area:

I wouldn't like a daughter of mine to marry a coloured person. If they're educated they're all right ... There's some dreadful white people aren't there? Some cruel white people. I mean, if you're cruel and ignorant and repulsive ...

On this cue the rest of the cast entered dressed as members of the Klu Klux Klan and chanted in a general crescendo:

We represent the whites and so are superior.
We are all members of the Klu Klux Klan.
We must get rid of the black man, he is inferior,
And this country was made by God for the white man ...

Their movement echoed that of our opening number but as they closed in chanting *Kill, Kill, Kill* the tension was broken by the coloured man jumping up as though from a nightmare and walking down to the front of the stage to address the audience directly. In the actor's own words:

The last speech was taken very slowly. We were now hoping every member of the audience was with us. Our Pakistani friend removed his mask and explained that he was not black or brown, but white. Or was he? A pinky, pasty yellow would have been nearer. We wanted them to see the situation in which this man found himself, simply because he was coloured. Having finally reached our objective, the audience did not know what to think. We all joined hands and sang 'We shall overcome'. The cast tended to judge their success each evening by looking at the faces of the audience as they left the auditorium. Had we made them think? Had we told them anything? Anything to which they had previously been unaware or to which they had turned a blind eye? Had we told them something of themselves? We would never know. We just hoped that we had, in fact, said something.

It is evident from this sort of comment that the greatest value of the exercise to the pupils lay in making a protest about injustice and in being committed about something. They had probed quite deeply into a serious problem and because they had thought about it adults had been obliged to think about it too. The art side was carefully supervised by the Art teacher who insisted that the sets and costumes be designed and made by members of the group – two of the quiet girls who could not be prevailed upon to act on stage but who willingly took on this task. All the rest of the group took part in the show together with another thirty or so pupils from the fourth year upwards. Not one complaint was received about the material. This was due, I think to the obvious sincerity of the players. It is worth adding a comment on the attitude of the headmaster who gave every encouragement possible and had sufficient confidence in both the pupils and staff concerned to allow them to work unhindered and uncensored.

Having learned a great deal we now wished to expand the scope of our work. We had learned a lot about putting a play together and about being committed to something, but we did not feel, on reflection, that we as a group had written enough original material. We had used Benet's poetry – why could we not write our own? And why could we not write much more of our music instead of using other people's?

During the second year of this two-hour session, held this time for thirty pupils from both fifth and sixth forms, our aim was again to explore relationships between art and drama but we were able to expand much more because we had a movement teacher and the head of the music department to help. This immediately added a whole new dimension to the work. Other members of staff gave generously of their spare time when required. By utilizing these elements we intended to try to make up an original dramatic presentation based on the sixteenth-century Spanish conquest of Mexico and perform it as the school play.

As we wished to compile a completely different sort of presentation, we were careful to make the first session as interesting as possible. With thirty pupils the approach obviously had to be different. We decided to start from art again and this time we looked at sculpture, its concern with the human form, its inspiration from landscape and natural phenomena and its statement through the artist on them. We discussed the visual and tactile experience of sculpture by using quotations from Henry Moore:

Our sense of sight is always closely associated with our sense of touch.

A child learns about roundness from handling a ball far more than from looking at it. Even if we touch things with less immediate curiosity as we grow older, our sense of sight remains closely allied to our sense of touch.

My belief is that no matter what advances we make in technology, and in the controlling of nature and so on, the real basis of life is in human relationships. It is through them that we are happy or unhappy, and that we fulfil ourselves, or we don't. There is a great deal more to be done with 3-dimensional form as a means of expressing what people feel about themselves and nature and the world around them. But I don't think that we shall, or should, ever get far away from the thing that all sculpture is based on in the end: the human body.

We then asked the group to explore some of these ideas by touching textures around the room and outside, feeling a brick, a blackboard, a wall, door and glass. Having done this we asked them to create shapes with the stacking chairs, at the same time listening to shapes and textures in sound provided by electronic music. The human jungle, fungus attacking an object, childbirth, suffering, scaffolding, and even the famous 'Kop' terraces of the Liverpool football ground were thus created. The children then used these constructions as starting points for several movement sequences and this sort of expression seemed both logical and natural for them. This being so it was next suggested that the experience of seeing, touching and moving could be extended by the use of colours and shapes. Many cut-out shapes in paper were given out and we started off with the stage in darkness. The first movement of Bartok's *Concerto for Orchestra* was played and various lighting effects were introduced, the shapes being used to catch and reflect the light whilst the bodies moved and the whole gave a kaleidoscopic effect, constantly changing, of the elements we had discussed earlier. We ended the first session by suggesting that we should work towards a school play based on the conquest of Mexico, which would involve the whole group in considerable research, not only factual, but in the exploration of techniques in movement and drama. A number of books were recommended, and the pupils were urged to begin reading as soon as possible.

In the next session we decided to concentrate on the acquisition of techniques of making percussive sounds and rhythms as a stimulus for movement. The pupils were asked to clap in simple and compound rhythms and to use their voices rhythmically. Then simple instruments were introduced, initially a number of off-cuts of wood of various shapes and sizes, borrowed from the woodwork room. Different sounds and rhythms were explored with these and then more instruments were introduced; maracas and their derivatives – tin shakers, different types of drum, cymbals, guitar, gong, piano, etc. After more exploration we asked for ideas on which to experiment. They suggested a thunderstorm and some time was spent in trying to evoke one using as much variety as we could. We then thought that if the group could move around with these instruments using them as we had used the chairs in the previous session the result might be more interesting. Small rostra were set out on the floor of the hall, steps were placed in front of the stage to link the different levels. As the sounds increased in volume and intensity and the lighting changed the individuals and groups began to move. The result was quite ritualistic and a certain sensitivity began to emerge as the pupils began to explore the possibilities of sound and light together. We rounded off the session by reading some quotations from Antonin Artaud's *Le Théâtre et son Double*:

Cries, groans, apparitions, surprises, theatricalities of all kinds, magic beauty of costumes taken from certain ritual models; resplendent lighting, incantational beauty of voices, the charms of harmony, rare notes of music, colours of objects, physical rhythm of movements whose crescendo and decrescendo will accord exactly with the pulsation of music and movements familiar to everyone, concrete appearances of new and surprising objects, masks, effigies yards high, sudden changes of light, the physical action of light which arouses sensations of heat and cold . . .

Musical instruments will be treated as objects and as part of the set.

There is, besides, a concrete idea of music in which the sounds make their entrance like characters.

It was pointed out to the pupils that they had been working on these lines in a very small way and that now they were aware of the possibilities we should explore them more fully.

For the third session we recapitulated some of the points covered in the first two sessions and discussed the many ideas which had arisen from them. This was followed by a discussion about the basic elements of the Aztec religion – human sacrifice and sun-worship – which provided the basis for a movement session. Acting on various suggestions from the group we built up rostra on the stage and in the hall for the different levels needed. In order to achieve an eerie quality we experimented with the coloured lights, suspending different objects, ladders, pieces of Dexian, in front of the cyclorama and succeeded in getting many different three-coloured shadows. Three girl 'sacrifices' were placed on a rostrum on the ground floor. A crowd gathered round, forming a sculptured group. Two 'priests' wearing masks stood on the highest stage level, enacting ritualistic movements with the hands, then moving down slowly and menacingly towards the victims. Two of them managed to escape, leaving one caged by the crowd who opened only to allow the priests to take her for sacrifice. The crowd gradually moved forward while the priests re-enacted the ritual slaughter. Then the body was carried in procession and offered as propitiation to the rising sun which gradually increased in intensity.

We decided the following week to try to make up a play using techniques and ideas suggested by our previous work. Our aim was to use the work done in this preliminary play in the same way that an artist would use a sketch as a basis for a later painting. In view of the success of the Bristol Old Vic's cast during their tour of schools with *The Great Train Robbery* we thought we would take an equally immediate and interesting story, the murder of the three policemen by Harry Roberts and his accomplices. It was first necessary to make the factual outline quite clear. For this we read a newspaper cutting of the hearing of two of the men concerned in the case. A variety of ways and means of production were discussed and an outline of the sequence leading to the murder evolved. We started with two contrasting scenes showing the relaxed, happy atmosphere of the policemen, ironically wishing that they could see some action, and the tension of the three criminals plotting to release a jailed prisoner from Wormwood Scrubs. Gradually the two groups moved towards each other, a movement sequence of the shooting came next, followed by the escape. Then came TV and radio accounts of the shooting and the hunt was on. People on the spot were interviewed by police. The first break came – one of the men was captured and interviewed. Another went to Scotland where we imagined he hid out with his mother. Then he was captured. This left Harry Roberts. As the group continued the chase the commentators changed the scene of the manhunt. Epping Forest, Bristol and Ireland became centres of the search.

Some scenes worked very well and were fluent in speech and movement, others were unsuccessful. Where different techniques are being used and mixed together it is impossible to say what will work until it has been tried practically. It is of equal importance to the children that they should act both good and bad sequences, the value of the work being that they learn to distinguish between them and to be self-critical. In this way standards are raised and inferior work jettisoned.

We met the following week to discuss ways and means of improving the play and to introduce new ideas for our Mexican drama. Many points were raised. An interesting opening to the play was needed, perhaps a narrator, or a ballad-singer; could the contrast between police and criminals be heightened by differences in speech; would verse be appropriate? Several plays were discussed in connection with these points – *Oedipus Rex* and Greek choruses generally; the opening of *Romanoff and Juliet*. The discussion was stimulating and it was evident that the group had gained a great deal of useful experience from this 'blueprint'.

For the rest of the afternoon we had invited a member of the Spanish department to use his wide knowledge of sixteenth-century Mexico, much of it gained from original Spanish sources, to talk to the group about the factual background of the Spanish conquest. In the course of an hour's talk he outlined the relevant legends and historical facts, starting with the legend of Cuatlicueh the Earth Mother, the birth of Huitzlipochtli and the eventual driving out of Quetzalcoatl. Then, basing the events upon Bernal Diaz' narrative, the main points of Cortes' voyage to Mexico were outlined and the eventual death of Montezuma. The amount of research and time taken was greatly appreciated by the children who seemed well aware of the interest shown by many different people.

We completed a full afternoon's work with a twenty-minute film from the British Film Institute on pre-Colombian Mexican art, which showed many examples of Aztec and Toltec sculptures, pottery and artifacts.

The first five sessions had led from the dissemination of ideas to the difficult task of working out a play. This had to be kept to a fairly tight story line, using several theatrical devices, and had to have a clear and deep delineation of character. It could also suggest modern colonial parallels.

In the sixth session we decided to begin serious work on the chosen topic. We went first to the music room to explore some of the elements of improvisation in music, this time creating patterns and melodies based on the five-tone scale which is the basis of most primitive music. We wished now to use melody as well as rhythm and to develop this with our dramatic work. The most suitable starting-point seemed to be the legendary basis of the whole story as there are so many echoes of it in the factual account. In the beginning all was darkness until Cuatlicueh, the Earth Mother, gave birth to the moon and stars. Whilst she was sweeping the Earth one day a ball of feathers fell from the sky. She put them into her girdle and so became pregnant. When they heard of Cuatlicueh's pregnancy the moon and stars were incensed and began to arm against her. The child grew inside her and shouted against the other elements. At the moment of confrontation between the moon, stars and earth the child was born in full armour. His name was Huitzli-pochtli, the god of the sun. At his birth the moon and stars were put to flight. The Aztecs were the chosen people of this god and were told that human sacrifice and blood were the only means for ensuring the continuance of his ascendancy. This became the central focus of their worship and continued until another god, Quetzalcoatl, railed against it. Quetzalcoatl, another sun god, was driven away towards the East, but before he left he said he would return again, in a One-Reed year (which occurred every 52 years in the Aztec calendar) to stop this barbaric practice and establish himself. The year of Cortes' arrival, 1519, was a One-Reed year ...

How was this legend to be presented dramatically? The majority suggested a disembodied voice to speak it whilst movement and lighting were used to heighten the effect. We asked for contributions in biblical style, verse, and simple prose, and stopped for half an hour to allow everyone to explore and talk about their ideas more fully and to write down any contributions. Written accounts of various styles and of excellent quality were quickly made available for us to work on. This is the version we chose and which eventually provided the opening to the actual play:

> And in a place long ago and o'er the sea
> Was nothing but great darkness and void.
> Till came Cuatlicueh, Goddess of the Earth,
> Called 'She of the Snaky Skirts'.
> Then came the stars born with the moon
> And with them the wondrous joy of life.
> Suddenly one day from the heavens there came
> Feathers, feathers, feathers,
> Beauteous in a multitudinous mass,
> One of which she did gently place in her girdle
> And was thereof happily with child.
> Rejoicing, she awaited the birth in peace.
>
> Thunderous rage and anger of contempt
> Came from the stars and moon because of this.
> And then 'twas that Cuatlicueh gave birth to Huitzlipochtli,
> Who, in shiny armour clad was the Sun,
> Born to drive back the forces of Darkness.
> Thus followed battle bloody 'twixt Dark and Light.
>
> Came then the Aztec peoples to this land
> In great procession proud.

Looked they upon this battle of blood,
And being afeared by the dark of Night
Took side with the warm, earth-comforting sun.
Thus, determining to spill blood for the daylight cause,
They undertook with ceremony great and dignity high
A religion of blood-letting human sacrifice.

'Stop!', said a voice, heavy with horror and tears,
At the sight of sacrifice so bloody.
'Twas the voice of Quetzalcoatl,
Come to redeem these people from such a religion.
The Aztec people stood petrified, their faces frightened.
This gentle god from the East
Bathed in a glory of peaceful words.

But the Sun God, Huitzlipochtli, infused the Aztecs
With his need for their blood,
And they grew in hatred.
So much so that they advanced with malice calculated
Upon Quetzalcoatl, to get him gone.
And so, this God of Gentleness, not wishing to spill blood,
Fled back towards the Eastern Sea.

QUETZALCOATL: I shall return in a One-Reed year. It will be a time of great
tribulation for the Aztec people.

The group was divided into those who wanted to move, make music,
arrange lighting, narrate, etc., and started to work, using this text. As a
result, some semblance of the style of presentation began to emerge and we
had provided a foundation on which the play could be built. It quickly
became obvious that colour and costume were to be of great importance.

Well aware of the difficulties likely to arise with the enormous task of
compiling a play we had invited Charles Wood, the playwright and film
scriptwriter to school for the next session. As the writer of the Beatles' film
Help! and the award-winning film *The Knack*, his work had a quality and
immediacy which had greatly impressed those of the children who had seen
these films. Mr Wood was concerned that rather than lecture to the children
they should talk to him as much as possible. He talked about his own background as a writer and his particular interest at that time in writing about
his own experiences from 17 to 23. The children warmed quickly to this
sincere and informal approach and asked many questions: How did he go
about writing a play? How was he treating the epic theme of 'The Charge
of the Light Brigade' on which he was working at the time? What was the
writer's relationship with the director in theatre or cinema? Would he adapt
someone else's work? What did he think of blanket titles such as Theatre of

Cruelty? What was his opinion of critics, audiences and censorship? What could he tell us about Peter Brook's methods in rehearsals of *US*? They were all sympathetically considered and answered in as much detail as possible. This stimulating afternoon enabled us to see more clearly what we were about. Charles Wood showed that a sincere, deep approach to any form of artistic activity was the most important starting-point and though there were great disappointments few things were as satisfactory as writing something original which required careful thought and research.

In the eighth session we returned to our theme and a violent argument flared up concerning the projected use of a narrator. It was agreed that the character should be Bernal Diaz, the chronicler, but his manner of delivery and style of speech were strenuously contested. Some were for a Brechtian style of narration, direct to the audience in everyday language. The others insisted that he should retain some of the flowery character of sixteenth-century language. The paths gradually converged and different people were asked to provide the contrast of styles. The main protagonists were given a week in which to polish their different speeches. This problem having been resolved for the moment the group was again divided into those who wished to work on music and those who wanted to improvise with speech. The musicians went off to work on background music to a poem, here quoted in part, written by one of the girls in her spare time:

> We are alive, but slip every second
> Towards the everlasting sleep.
> Peace is quiet, still and long
> Lulling voices in the wind.
> Yet even the slightest sound can
> Penetrate the stillness:
> The rising of a restless lark, the
> Fleeting of its lofty wings, from soaring
> Branch to sky.
> The cracking of a twig underfoot,
> The drizzle of a raindrop, touching
> A weightless vein.
> Anything can shatter peace, and
> Make it as an everlasting hell.
>
> So is war, the ruination of mankind.
> This killer of men's souls can filter its disease
> Into every piece of every limb.
> The sickening foe can slither round the
> Heart, and lighten frozen brains.
> The thought of death can spur a nation,
> Yet dying shatters courageous hearts.

War is a valiant word. Every time
Its glory spreads a glow upon the earth
Men struggle in their helplessness, and beg
To be an army strong.
They are just like children with a ball,
Who will lead, and who will fall
Into the last of line?
Honour, Glory, whisper dreaming heroes
Of self-joy.
Blazing eyes feel the freedom of
Majesty, the glory of touching the sandal
Of their mighty leader, the great Cortes . . .

In the play these lines were divided between the Spanish soldiers and a chorus of Aztec women who commented on war. The rest of the group in this session were divided into pairs and were asked to imagine that they were waiting to be interviewed for a job. While waiting they questioned the other person to find out as much about him as possible. In this way 'characters' were developed. Later, a third person was introduced but he would divulge no information about himself, thus breeding suspicion. The group was then asked to make a short scene on 'Suspicion' or 'Intrigue'.

Having now decided that our first scene should be a poetic evocation of the Aztec legend, we needed to make a smooth transition to Cuba, where the Spanish element was introduced. Taking Diaz as our link we had to establish the first of the scenes introducing the Spaniards and to plan our line of approach. Our earlier improvisations helped in this direction. The choice of Cortes as leader of the expedition to Mexico was riddled with intrigue. The relative passage of Diaz' narrative was read and the group began work.

At the end of the afternoon we looked at some of the different approaches and, as these varied considerably, some interesting discussion, occasionally flaring into argument, ensued. Uppermost in all this was the question of style which we finally decided should be kept fluid and natural for the moment, but should be thought about and worked upon very carefully later on when our command of the subject and characters became more expert.

The next session began with a discussion of some of the problems raised the previous week. The problem of the narrator's speech was solved when the group unanimously accepted this version:

NARRATOR: I am called Bernal Diaz del Castillo, a man of humble birth, but proud to be named such a name. My speech is chilled and my body shakes, yet, lowly as I am, my mind is filled with a great wonder – a fable that is imprinted within my soul so heavily that I cannot erase it. My eyes are leaden, yet I can still see with a clear light the amazing tale that makes me an important man . . .

We read through and noted certain scenes which took place in Cuba from Diaz – the choice of Cortes; Velasquez' doubts after choosing Cortes; a buffoon speaks to Velasquez; Cortes' reaction to Velasquez' attempts to depose him. Some of the group undertook to work on these scenes and to have ideas ready for the fifth-year pupils when they arrived after first lesson. The artistic director of the Bristol Old Vic Company and an inspector of schools were visitors for the afternoon. They participated in discussion and helped the group in many ways. At the end of the afternoon we watched some of the scenes and had a lively discussion about them.

The pupils were gradually becoming more confident in their work and were already beginning to probe deeper into motives and relationships. On the other hand some pupils were being overshadowed by others and it was most important that the opportunities for the weaker ones should be as great as those for the stronger actors. Music, design and writing would probably provide adequate outlets for such pupils as we moved on with the story. Perhaps the most pleasing feature of the course was the development of the group's critical faculties. The characters were discussed and analysed at length. Arguments were nearly always constructive and criticism was accepted by everyone. The groups listened carefully to each other, and their concentration while working was excellent. At all times they were genuinely concerned to raise their standards.

As we had now made a firm basis for the play it was obvious that our two-hour sessions would be quite inadequate for rehearsing and polishing the material. We decided to stay on until 6 p.m. on Thursday afternoons and to work on another two evenings besides. Auditions were held, open to fourth-year pupils and above. We were inundated with prospective actors and actresses and worked them in crowd scenes and movement sequences whilst some of the group took off the more talented ones and worked on scenes with them. From this time we found that we were able to speed up our progress. Whereas we had sometimes taken a whole afternoon to improvise one scene we began to be able to work out several in a rehearsal and polish them.

It would be impossible to describe the finished performance fully. The stage, covered in silver paper for Mexico, was at one end of the hall and a great pyramid, reaching nearly to the roof and made of scaffolding, was at the other. The action flowed between these focal points, often taking place in and around the audience, with banners, shields, costumes and lighting providing the colour and a great detachable sun-calendar dominating all with enormous flats depicting Aztec chronicle-paintings set up around the auditorium.

The action concerned Cortes' trip to Tenochtitlan and this took up most of the first act, culminating in his meeting with Montezuma and his acceptance as the god Quetzalcoatl. The second act looked closely at the relationship between Cortes and Montezuma set against the opulence of Mexico and the crusading zeal of the catholic Spaniards, and ended with the destruction of the city and a chorus of Aztec women lamenting:

> Death-struck people are left to weep
> In depths of dark despair.
> War has drummed its powerful beat
> But all for useless end.
> Destruction waved its fleshless hand;
> Now ashes lie upon the ground.
> There is nothing; nothing now.

As a performance it lacked pace, mainly because of the poetic quality we had stressed. It tended to be rather heavy-handed as we had been very serious about it and we should have used a lot more funny sequences to add variety. In fact, the sheer size of the conception almost defeated us, but not quite. To walk around the school at lunch-time and see the hundreds of pupils in the school making props, designing costumes, reading up facts, writing scenes and poetry, was an experience not to be missed. The highlight of the whole project, however, came during the performance when a mystery virus attacked practically the whole cast who just managed to stay on stage until their exit when they either fainted or became violently sick. At a most important point in the development of the story Cortes was forced to make an early exit and missed the next scene. One of the soldiers, a boy from a remedial department class, immediately took over, carried through a difficult scene with Montezuma and by the time Cortes had recovered had kept the play moving and earned the respect and admiration of the whole cast. That was a moment which all concerned will cherish and it told us quite clearly what this sort of work can accomplish. In fact we had all given as much to it as we possibly could. As one of the staff concerned said, 'I have never been stretched so much in my whole teaching career.'

Once again, the next year we decided to change our tack and work on more productions of less scope, and to tackle texts again. We thought that it might be interesting and useful to use the experience we had gained by working with younger children. As my wife had a class of primary school children who were good at music, we invited them to the school for an afternoon. They sang and played for us and we presented a ten-minute improvised play called *Prince Trevor and the Dragon's Tooth*. They liked this so much that they asked if we would take it to their school and show it. We agreed and then divided them into groups to work with us. The results were very interesting and it was surprising to see the rapport between the two sets of children. The next few weeks were spent in polishing *Prince Trevor* and making it into a half-hour play which we took to the primary school and showed very successfully.

For the school play we decided on a double bill – Aristophanes' *Peace* for those who wanted to work on a script, and an improvised work on the history of clowning from Caligula to the Goons called *Clowns*. The head of the music department wrote some Theodorakis-type music for the first, and we had a small circus-type band on stage for the second. They went down very well with the audience for both were gay and amusing, and we had again managed to do a lot of original work and research.

In the summer when Robert Kennedy was assassinated the group decided they would write a play about it. This was called *Guns!* and looked at violence in America. It was composed in rough form in one day. Additions were made, a definite structure was established, and the first performance was given in July 1968. A discussion was held for both the cast and audience afterwards which the actors regarded as essential to promote direct audience participation, and because the play deliberately had no end on stage. The whole idea was completely that of the pupils and the result was so interesting and controversial that we were asked to show it at a national conference on drama and theatre, where it had a very mixed reception.

The involvement of the group, however, did not end here. After *The Conquest of Mexico* we tended to put on six productions a year at the school. The first was the house drama evening, run entirely by the pupils; the second a pantomime, extended from our plays for primary school children, with lots of music and participation; the third was the school play; later came the fourth-year drama club presentation, generally produced by a member of staff; then the junior school play – often a musical such as *The Midnight Thief* or *The Story of Lieutenant Cockatoo*; and finally a short sixth-form production. With so much activity going on it was essential to delegate a lot of the production work and the group delighted in taking on the responsibility for some of the rehearsals with younger children.

My final production was John Arden's *The Happy Haven*, a difficult play and one which would not have been feasible for the cast had they not already had a great deal of experience of improvisation.

Lawrence Weston School stands on a large housing estate on the outskirts of Bristol. It is a working-class area with no cinemas or theatres. The school provides the estate with almost all its culture. The pupils all come from the estate and it is interesting to note that in the past few years young people went from the school to universities, drama colleges, art colleges and colleges of education, all to study some aspect of drama or stage design. This would have been unthinkable had it not been for our Thursday afternoon sessions – billed as 'Recreation afternoon'. There must be a moral there somewhere.

A *scripted ballad opera*

STEPHEN and HILARY TUNNICLIFFE

Here the approach to the school play is not from movement or improvisation but from a script, arrived at by a team of senior pupils working with the producer.

Newtown is a relatively isolated country town, the nearest professional theatre being more than fifty miles away. The High School became a fully co-educational comprehensive school only a year before this production was staged, but Stephen Tunnicliffe had good though conventional traditions of school drama and music from its constituent schools on which to build.

The project began experimentally as an out-of-school activity, but soon gathered impetus and took its place as the main dramatic activity in the school year. Contrary to many adults' taste in drama, children generally prefer their plays to have clear moral overtones. In the play that emerged the tense situations and the verbal punch left considerable room for genuine acting, and the detached figure of the ballad singer added a refreshingly ancient, almost Bardic touch, interpreting and commenting upon the action as it unfolded. Hilary Tunnicliffe emphasized this Welsh-ness in her wise decision to mix traditional and original music, both of which formed an integral part of the final production.

The power of this play lies in its relevance to both actors and audience and their participation in a contemporary social situation, terrible in its nearness. The language lacks the polish of a West End production but retains an honesty which reflects the writers' own outlook on their environment.

Stephen Tunnicliffe read English at Queen Mary College, London. He has written libretti for various composers and is a joint editor of *English in Practice* (Cambridge, 1971). He had had wide experience of drama in schools, and is at present head of the English department of Newtown High School.

Hilary Tunnicliffe studied music at the Royal Academy of Music, London. She has written and arranged music for many school productions, including Yeats' *Countess Cathleen* and three Shakespeare plays; more recently, she has written a stage play. She is on the music staff of Salop Education Authority.

The school play as an institution has had many critics. It tends to be an opportunity for the school to show off, it encourages the restriction of acting opportunities to a few stars, it fosters an undue attention to showiness in production, often at the expense of more worth-while matters – the school-master–producer with a weather eye on his public and his governors may be tempted to choose inferior, even meretricious material because it is easier to handle slickly. All these are valid criticisms, and many drama and English teachers would argue that they point to the need for abandoning the idea of a single major production in favour of several less ambitious but more widely spread activities.

On the other hand it is easier to engage staff and student support for a single production; moreover, most schools have expensive capital tied up in lighting equipment, sound-effects, sets and so on, which it is wasteful not to use, and which cannot be fully exploited except through a major production. There are compensations, too. The enthusiasm engendered, and the high standards often achieved, do tend to spill over into clubs and societies, play-reading groups and the like.

I was faced with this familiar dilemma at Newtown High School. The schools that amalgamated to form this 800-strong country comprehensive had good traditions of school drama – an unbroken succession of Shakespeare plays at the boys' grammar school, for instance, extending over several years – and to break totally with the idea of a school play would have destroyed much good will. On the other hand, in a school like this one must never give the impression that drama is exclusively for the 'grammar stream' – the name is not used, but the idea dies hard. I decided therefore for my first production to experiment.

My aims were, first, to present something that would be intelligible to the majority of the school while still being serious drama; secondly, to enlist as wide a range of talents as possible, especially from the more prominent and successful school activities such as music; and thirdly, to make the best possible use of existing talent and good will. All these seemed to point in one direction – to a home-made, or do-it-yourself play. Happily, the idea of writing or even group-creating one's own play is gaining acceptance.

The genre of ballad opera appealed to me for several reasons. In the first place it left room for both naturalistic drama and a more formal and stylized approach – a great advantage when your end-product is dependent on the way it takes shape. Secondly, it gave scope for music without dictating the extent to which music was involved. The school is particularly fortunate in having a strong tradition of instrumental music, largely due to the enthusiasm of one lively teacher. The choral side, on the other hand, was weak at the time. Thirdly, I feel, with so many others, that the pervasive influence of Brecht has been an immense stimulus to creative drama, and I wanted to harness some of it in a school context. It is no accident that performances of *Caucasian Chalk Circle* have become so frequent in schools, and I have seen an excellent production of *Galileo* in a medium-sized comprehensive school with only a small drama department. Finally, my own involvement in music-making was an advantage – I was one of the instrumentalists in the 'orchestra' – and I was fortunate in being able to enlist my wife in the venture, she being a practical musician with considerable experience of writing for drama.

There happened to be two sixth-formers in my English set – a boy and a girl – who had their sights firmly set on drama schools. These two, with another girl, agreed to form a script team with me, and in the spring term we set to work. We started with what is perhaps the most pressing local problem in mid-Wales – depopulation – and worked out a play-theme using the town–country conflict as central. To this the script-writers decided to add the more familiar conflict of parents versus children.

It may be helpful here to describe the script team. Eleri-Ann Thomas is the daughter of a primary school headmaster in Newtown, a lively and original girl with considerable gifts both as a writer and as a musician. Hers was the most original mind in the team, and I found her enthusiasm and talent a tremendous help. She recorded in writing her impressions of the venture for me, and I shall be quoting from this first-hand account. The second girl, Jennifer Lewis, was the daughter of a local farmer – not so instinctively aware of dramatic possibilities as Eleri-Ann, but with an acute ear for the tone of natural dialogue. She contributed what one might call the everyday appeal, and much of the natural turn of phrase, to the script. Jennifer was also musical, playing the violin in the school orchestra. Peter Murphy was the son of the local police inspector. He was the most dedicated of the three to all things connected with the stage, and his lively and vigorous participation was a great stimulus to me and to the other two. An actor with a natural stage presence, and with useful experience in school productions, he brought to the team an invaluable knowledge of stage technique, much of it based also on perceptive theatre going. Naturally, the two aspirants to drama school had forceful ideas about the parts they would like to take. I was fascinated to see the way they responded to the stimulus of having to create from scratch parts for themselves.

We gave ourselves plenty of time, and it was as well that we did so. I would advise any teacher venturing on a similar experiment to allow two clear terms for preliminary work before actual rehearsals start – unless they tackle the whole job the other way round, building up situations and plot from improvised episodes. Our first discussions concerned the chosen themes, and from these we imperceptibly moved into talking about the main characters. Eleri-Ann puts it neatly: 'The basic theme of depopulation in Montgomeryshire encompassed two other important themes which came out strongly in the final production – the antagonism between youth and the older generation, and the continual rift between town life and country life.'

As in most forms of writing we found ourselves forced again and again to simplify. Our first outline of the story, when it emerged, seemed trite and obvious, and only began to be acceptable when we faced the actual task of writing dialogue. The scriptwriters, like most sixth-formers, had strong views about what they considered phoney or corny; however, they discovered – and this was one of the worth-while by-products of the venture – that the superficial condemnation along these lines that passes for independence of thought amongst teenagers was not a reliable guide when it came to producing rather than receiving. As writers they were on their mettle, and they responded to it well. I can think of no better way to start original writing, or to come to a real understanding of what creative writing (that much abused phrase) really involves, than to set about producing work within such a context, where both the actors – the executants of their work – and the public, before whom it would be performed, were a part of their own immediate environment.

Our first method, whereby each member of the team wrote separate versions of a scene, then we read and discussed and combined them, had its disadvantages; but it was most helpful in the initial stages. 'I realized very soon [writes Eleri-Ann] that we all had the same feel for words and could criticize each other's work constructively.' In particular it helped the team to develop a group style, which enabled individual scriptwriters to do whole scenes later without risk of diverging from the agreed characterization. This submerging of individual styles is no bad discipline for fledgling authors; it has a counterpart these days in the professional field, when authors as individual as Stan Barstow or Alan Plater can work happily and with integrity at episodes in *Z Cars* or *Softly, Softly*.

So far the work was developing simply as a straight play. My original idea had been to give the music much more prominence, and to have the main characters as ready to sing as to speak, but this was, I now believe, a mistake, and I did not press it. A teacher entering into this kind of enterprise has always to choose between on the one hand imposing his own conception of the work, stimulating others through his keenness and singlemindedness to work within the structure he has created; and on the other coming to it with relatively fluid ideas, and convincing his team that the final structure is their joint responsibility, and that their ideas on the shape it will take are as valid as his own. I believe both methods have their advantages. In the first the end-product may be more daring, more original, perhaps more ambitious, and it will bear the mark of a single personality. It may have been that I felt I could not measure up to such demands, but I chose in fact the latter method. The ballad opera concept was accepted, but in a modified form. Indeed, except for the ballad singer's part, with her direct contact with the audience and her external control over the characters there were few departures from realism, the most notable being the scenery, and the final appearance of Ed in the role of sardonic observer rather than actor at the end of the play.

On her role as ballad singer Eleri-Ann makes these observations:

I wanted an informal, relaxed tone so that I could win the audience over immediately. Once this was achieved the possibilities were endless. I could point to an individual, I could address a group, I could lead them along the right lines of thought ...

The ballad singer's role was an excellent opportunity for achieving a real player–audience contact. This, and the use of a prologue and epilogue, appealed to me more than anything else, because it was completely free and could bring the audience directly into the heart of the play ... I think the audience appreciated the fact that I would sometimes dismiss the players myself, or sit with the audience to view the action ... From my very first line I tried to get near to my audience, and I could sense their delight when I mentioned a familiar local shop, or picked on someone in the second row ...

Each performance was new and different and exciting, and each time I was addressing a different audience so that I was able to play my part in a way that suited my audience. The whole atmosphere could change, and with each change I learnt something new.

However passive one intends to be, there are points where one is bound to give some lead, simply to counteract the sheer inexperience of the team. One such point was in determining the basic verse-form of the ballad singer's linking comments. They had to lead naturally into or out of the ballads themselves, so prose was out of the question. We eventually worked on the basis of a loose four-stress blank verse. It proved adaptable enough for our purposes, especially as Eleri-Ann, who wrote the bulk of what she was to perform, had a good rhythmic sense, and could bring out the verse-element without obscuring the immediacy of the colloquial tone adopted. The opening and closing choruses probably illustrate this most clearly:

(*The opening scene is a field. There are one or two bales of hay, and a stack of bales. Hot sun, and stillness.*)

BALLAD SINGER (*sings*):
>
> There is a meadow in the morning –
> Sickened by the silence –
> Through the hedge the town is calling,
> Up the roadway, round the hill.
>
> In the meadow there's a haystack –
> Sickened by the silence –
> Through the stack the town is turning,
> Up the roadway, round the hill.
>
> By the haystack there are people –
> Sickened by the silence –
> Through their eyes the town is shining
> Up the roadway, round the hill.

(*speaks*):
You've heard tonight's entertainment called
A ballad opera. Right? Well, I'm
The ballad singer. Words and music
Are both my province. Say it with music,
Say it in words. The world's a stage,
Said Jaques – but I don't agree.
My stage is here, and you are there
Audience, spectators at a show. Bored?
Amused, are you? Curious perhaps,
Looking forward to seeing Philip or Ann,
Pat or Colin, strutting it out
For a couple of hours – and a coffee-break,
We mustn't forget the coffee-break ... (*etc.*)

(*The final scene is outside the cottage that is to become the new youth centre. At the end, the babble of voices dies down as the ballad singer enters. She speaks.*)

There's nothing left for me to say.
There you have it, our ballad opera,
Finished – ended – over.
We've tried to say a lot of things,
Things that needed to be said.
We've tried to give you the very feelings that we felt.
But when you leave this hall tonight
Remember just one thing – that nothing
In our show tonight has got to be accepted.
We made it real, we made it live,
But what you think, and what you feel –
The things you've learnt, or haven't learnt –
They're your concern, they're your affair.
Your conclusions are yours, not ours.

We hope you will think, we hope you have cause,
And now we ask for your applause.

These opening and closing passages, and the excerpts quoted later, must be read within the context for which they were intended – performance by and to country-dwellers. A city school would undoubtedly produce a script entirely different in tone, range of reference and so on; and the impermanence of the work is the price one must pay for its immediacy – a point that comes out clearly again in the discussion of the music. The area served by the school is fully rural; the working community are largely dependent on farming and forestry, apart from a few small factories, and attitudes and behaviour reflect both the stability which forms the positive side of local culture, and the narrow parochialism and resistance to change that are perhaps more often associated with country life – though they are not the exclusive properties of country-dwellers.

There is no local professional theatre, so most people's ideas of drama are shaped by such productions as are staged by the amateur dramatic societies. I do not intend this in any disparaging sense; lively societies like the one at Newtown – which has recently accumulated enough funds to make its own very attractive little theatre – are doing very valuable service, and undoubtedly keep the idea of theatre alive in country districts more positively than the most sophisticated television productions. On the other hand, the plays chosen often fall short of what one might call serious or worth-while drama, and the pervasive influence of cliché-ridden dialogue and stereotyped characterization is hard to combat, almost impossible to escape completely. I believe it is to similar, rather suspect influences, that we owe the current vogue in 'musicals' – a genre that demands unusual creative gifts if it is to escape the easy sentimentality, trite harmonization and syrupy melodies of such compilations as *Oliver*, for instance.

Our production took place in the school hall, a large rectangular building without distinction, but with remarkably good acoustics. It has a fairly roomy stage at one end, built behind the usual proscenium arch. Thanks to a keen member of staff the lighting and sound arrangements, built into a gallery above one side of the stage, are well above average, and allowed for considerable variety in stage effects. I should have liked to increase the sense of contact with the audience by means of an apron stage, but had to be content with giving the ballad singer a small apron stage where she sat for some scenes, at other times moving freely in and out of the set. The small orchestra was placed in the auditorium to one side of the stage, and screened from the audience. On reflection I think it might have been better to have the musicians in full view of the audience, but this would have aggravated the problem of balance between soloist and instruments, which was difficult enough already, the hall being fairly resonant.

We set our minds firmly against the traditional creaking box set so beloved of old-time woodwork masters, in favour of light movable structures – a street-lamp, a set of steps, bales of straw – designed to barely suggest a scene, used in association with cyclorama and drapes and an abstract pattern on the side flats. My own early experience of school plays had developed in me a horror of the front curtain used to conceal nameless rumblings ill-disguised by scratchy gramophone records, so we dispensed with curtains altogether. The audience responded well to the change, and many of them reported that they had enjoyed watching the skill of the stage staff while listening to the ballad singer or musicians. Another advantage of this method is that back-stage helpers feel more involved when they actually appear, and children who could never act can still have the opportunity of demonstrating their skill in public.

The costumes were no problem, except for the ballad singer. For the others it was merely a matter of keeping a watchful eye on colour, and avoiding distracting clashes of style. The ballad singer had to look different, yet still 'mod', and we eventually fixed on a black pyjama suit with a gold sleeveless leotard.

The action of the play takes place in the small village of Pentre'r Meirw (Village of the Dead), and in Bethnal Green, London. Mrs Jordy and her son take a cottage in Pentre, and Ed soon senses the boredom of the village teenagers at the slow pace of village life. He is equally disenchanted with his mother's choice of home, so having won over a lively farmer's daughter, Jackie, persuades her and her three friends, Ruth, Andy and Tich, to make a bid for freedom by running away to London. Once there they find a place to live in the East End, and manage to get jobs, with the exception of Andy.

After the initial glamour wears off the teenagers begin to pull apart. Andy sets off for home in disgust, Jackie and Ed try to find a place to live on their own. In an attempt to raise the deposit for a flat Ed involves himself and Tich with a gang of drug-pushers. When Tich realizes where the easy money is coming from he tells the police, and the gang beat him up for his pains, forcing Ed to watch.

At this point one of the parents, Mr Harrow, arrives in town to persuade the others to return. He brings Jackie the news that her aunt is dead and her father has no one with him. That, together with Tich's injuries, helps to decide her to return to Pentre, and she is finally persuaded when Ed's sleazy acquaintance, the Stranger, tells her of Ed's lack of real feeling for her.

Back in the village the older people realize that something ought to be done for the youngsters, and, prompted by Jackie, who has discovered that Mrs Jordy wants to sell her cottage and return to London, they raise the funds to purchase it for conversion into a youth club. The play ends with the village teenagers at work on the cottage.

This bald outline of the plot gives some idea of the opportunities the script team succeeded in giving their actors. It had, in fact, been modified considerably, partly in response to what the actors made of it in rehearsal; alternatively the script team found themselves explaining and defending their ideas, as Eleri-Ann describes:

Rehearsals began while the script was still being written. In fact it was the other way around – we were still writing the script when rehearsals were under way. This was fine, in that anything that sounded too corny could be struck off, and of course a great deal was. A working script also had its disadvantages; more than once we had complaints from the actors about the unactable nature of a particular scene or dialogue. Ed protested frequently about his final speech, a crucial summing up of the whole play. All one could do was to assure him how effective it could be if he thought about it and got right inside the meaning. And he did.

The following notes on the cast and short excerpts from the script bring out clearly the dramatic possibilities inherent in the story as it finally took shape:

The cast – teenagers

JACKIE (Jacqueline Lawton): the eighteen-year-old only child of Mr Lawton, a farmer and widower. Pretty, wilful, bored with the monotony of country life. Lacking ambition but full of vitality. She has had her own way too much since her mother died.

ED (Edwin Jordy): also eighteen and an only child, living with his over-indulgent widowed mother in London up to the time the play opens. He has all the most recognizable 'undesirable' features of the teenage cult, long hair, leather jacket, off-hand manner, record of petty crime, powerful motor-bike.

RUTH and ANDY HARROW: aged sixteen and seventeen respectively. Children of the village schoolteacher, average, well-adjusted, prepared to follow rather than to lead.

TICH (Timothy Brown): seventeen, but small for his age. An orphan more or less adopted by Mr Lawton. He is a Londoner by birth, and a bit of a misfit in Pentre. Timid and ingratiating, keen on reading; shy, but anxious to be accepted.

Adults

TOM LAWTON (56): a farmer, somewhat uncommunicative, conservative and humourless.

AUNTIE CHRIS (Miss Christine Lawton): an older sister of Tom's who has acted as her brother's housekeeper since his wife died. Competent, fussy, keen on gossip.

MRS JORDY: about fifty, London-born, fairly recently widowed. Rather silly, and over-indulgent with her son, for whom she has little real understanding or sympathy.

MR and MRS HARROW (Paul and Vera): in their late forties. Straightforward, conventional, rather colourless.

PARSIE (Mrs Parslow): a comfortable, busy, cheerful cockney landlady in her fifties; friendly, sympathetic and understanding.

THE STRANGER: a sinister character from London's underworld – seedy, vicious and bitter. He controls his gang of toughs with ease.

THE GANG: three rough-necks, equipped with the usual array of knuckle-dusters, bicycle chains, etc.

Excerpt from scene 1 – part of the dialogue that follows the ballad singer's opening

JACKIE: ... I'll have to run this damn farm when Dad flakes out, I can see it coming.

RUTH: What about your auntie Chris?

JACKIE: Huh, I can't see old Chris doing it. She's all eager to help now, but once Dad goes she'll be off too – you just watch. I can see it now. There I'll be, a real old maid, getting up at five in the morning to feed the hens and milk the cows – God, what an awful thought.

RUTH: Oh, I don't know. I like to hear the people in the village talking about bringing in the hay and lambing and whether the weather will settle or not, and getting worried amongst themselves if one of their cows has caught pneumonia. There's something nice and cosy about farm life. The people are so – well, I dunno – so warm and homely kind of. It's a change from school talk anyway, and politics, and Vietnam.

JACKIE: Shut it, Ruth, you're up the creek. Like I said, it's all right for you – you don't live on a farm day in, day out. You don't know what it's like.

RUTH: Ah, stop moaning, Jackie – it's too hot to moan. You're too flipping self-piteous, you wallow in self-pity you do. Go to sleep, I'm trying to sunbathe.

JACKIE: Huh. (*She grunts miserably, closes her eyes for a moment.*) It beats me why the old man ever came here in the first place. (*Nobody answers. She sits up and tries again.*) I said it beats me ...

Excerpt from final scene – part of the dialogue before the ballad singer's closing words and music

(*The scene is outside Mrs Jordy's cottage. Jackie, Ruth, Andy and Tich are busy decorating the cottage and putting up shelves, etc.*)

JACKIE: Keep slapping it on – it's just right. (*She walks downstage. Pause. Work in progress.*) Well kids, it's all over. (*They all stop work and turn to look at her.*) It's in the past now – like a dream. It's as if it never really happened.

(*Spot picks out Ed dimly, downstage. He is leaning on a post or wall.*)

TICH: (*rubbing the plaster on his head*) It happened alright.

JACKIE: Poor old Tich. Never mind, we won't let it happen again, ever.

RUTH: I'm glad in a way. I'm glad we gave it a try. At least we know now, we know how lucky we really are. But I'm sure glad we're back home. I was beginning to miss them badly.

JACKIE: Me too. That's the trouble with people, you always end up missing them. You're right though. We owe a lot to Ed – specially me – and to Parsie and the

City. Even that filthy drug-peddlar taught me something. We've all learnt something, even if it was a hard lesson. (*Pause, She muses, the others stand silent.*) Orange! That's it, orange. The front of the soft drinks bar is going to be bright orange. (*The spell is broken. Renewed activity.*) See if you can mix a good vivid orange out of those two cans, Tich. Andy, get the step-ladder. Come on Ruth, grab a brush, I'll help you.

(*They all scatter. Jackie is about to follow Ruth and Tich into the cottage when Ed moves slowly forward. Jackie accepts his presence quite naturally. They are fairly close.*)

ED: So – we owe a lot to Ed, eh? But let's get 'im out of our system. Let's cover 'im up with new paint and pious phrases. It's so bloody easy, aint it?

JACKIE: Look, you've had your say, and you've had your chance. I wanted you, Ed. It was real, what I felt in that tatty room of Parsie's. Oh, I'm sorry, alright – honest, Ed. And you've still got part of me: I know, when I stop doing things, and being Jackie Lawton of Pentre. That's when you can make yourself felt. And all the longings, all what I felt about the city – you know, street lights in the rain and the rest of it. But was that really me, Ed? Where was I? Where am I?

ED: (*more bitter*) I, I, I! I can tell you where you are. Wrapped up in your own skin. And that's where each of us is – yeh, and the Stranger, and that dark-'aired tart at the club 'e let on to you about. And I'll tell you something. I like it that way, I like it, see? That's city life, that is. You're yerself. Pay your fare and no questions asked. And that's what I saw in you, Jackie (*gentler*) when I saw you in that hayfield. That stack behind you coulda bin Bethnal Green tube station. And now look at you! (*renewed bitterness*) What sort of a ruddy mother's meeting 'ave we got 'ere? Soft drinks bar – cor! And all chums together.

JACKIE: O.K. Laugh then. But let me tell you something too, Mister independent Edwin. You won't always get by with just paying a fare. I found that out when Auntie Chris died. You can kid yourself that you're alone – that you're your own boss – for just so long. And then something happens. (*She goes nearer him*). It's true, Ed, isn't it? You know it too. What about Tich when he got beaten up? And what about us, Ed? We've meant something to each other, haven't we?

(*She takes both his hands in hers, arms out, looking at him. There are noises, and finally shouts, from the others calling for Jackie.*)

ED: I ... maybe ... Jackie. (*As she drops his hands he holds them out, then slowly drops his arms and steps back into the shadow.*)

(*Ruth and Tich run in, calling Jackie.*)

RUTH/TICH: Jackie, Jackie. Come on, Jackie. A name, a name. What shall we call it? The club – what name shall we give it? ...

I believe that the production did repay the effort that had gone into it and prove a worth-while venture, and I put it forward as a sample of what is possible in an average country comprehensive school without outstanding facilities. By not setting one's sights too high one can achieve a good enough standard to make people feel they have participated in something memorable, and at the same time provide a vehicle for the few exceptional talents always to be found in good secondary schools.

One of these at Newtown was that of Eleri-Ann Thomas, and I should like to conclude with her words:

The play's growth over a period of twelve months was not only exciting and stimulating, but it taught me more about writing and acting in that period of time than in the whole of my school career. I can feel a great satisfaction in having written a play which turned out to be so worthwhile. It taught me more about people, because I explored human nature, and the reactions and motivations of people in certain situations. I learnt a great deal about the technicalities of production, and the disciplines necessary as well as the freedom available in acting and writing ... *Worlds Apart* was the most exciting thing that I have ever done.

THE MUSIC (H.T.)

Clearly the music needed to shoulder some of the dramatic load. It seemed necessary that some of it should be original, also that we should make use of traditional folk material, being part of the childhood memories of Welsh children. On studying several songs we found material for our purposes; threads of melody were strong enough, even in fragmentation, to stand the strains of contrapuntal treatment, and the rhythms, which were powerful and lively, promised a variety and strength of reinforcement to whatever pattern should emerge in our finished product. These tunes could only gain from an attempt to treat them in a harmonically enterprising manner.

There was little arbitrary decision-making about the score for *Worlds Apart*. Eleri-Ann Thomas, the ballad singer, was responsible for the words I was to use. She writes:

Ballads were placed at crucial points in the play, to clarify and simplify the action and to stress the implications of an act or scene. Out of five ballads, three used traditional Welsh melodies, one was a specially written pop song, and the fifth had a specially composed melody which became the theme from the overture throughout the play. Each ballad created a link with the basic theme of the play, and often the same tune would be repeated. Of the five songs I wrote the lyrics of two. The pop song was very exciting to write, but it took nearly a month to produce two verses and a chorus.

Songs or instrumental music were needed in certain places. Suggestions were made, considered, adopted or abandoned; times were calculated, cuts, extensions, repeats carried out. Any producer is aware of the problems involved. Our music was 'live' and the players very much a part of the production. We had five solo instrumentalists – violin, cello, bass, oboe and clarinet. Their individual parts were written for them, and they were good players, so the parts did not have to be too simple.

The Welsh tunes used were 'Robin Gogh', 'Robin Ddiog' (sometimes

known as 'Y Morwr'), and 'The Ash Grove'. Many more were suggested
but were rejected for one reason or another. One in particular – 'Cân Serch'
– was found to be productive of nothing but darkness and despondency,
whereas some of the others – 'Robin Gogh', for example – contained seeds
of rhythmic lightness which developed under treatment. I found sufficient
material in these three, together with an original tune (see Example 1,
'There is a Meadow') alive with possibilities from the arranger's point of
view.

EXAMPLE 1

The scriptwriters wrote the words for this, as they did for the three Welsh
tunes. The musicians wanted the tunes embodied in an entertaining overture, as well as being arranged so that they could accompany the words. The
combination of instruments in the 7-minute overture made possible a
genuine independence of parts and florid melodic treatment; most of the
material in it was suggested in some way by the songs themselves, and parts
of it were used elsewhere in the play.

When it came to rehearsals the ballad singer found that the unexpected
instrumental texture and the – to her – unfamiliar harmonic idiom made her
songs difficult to sing (see Example 2, 'Robin Gogh'). The accompaniments
were not starkly modern, neither were any of the discords uncomfortably
harsh; in fact they now appear to me to be lamentably orthodox, but this is
one great advantage of using original material. At the time of its use it is
adequate and evocative, being created for the job in hand; for another
occasion, for another set of children in a different place or for a different
group of instrumentalists the music would be different too. It was tailored
for the occasion, and those present agreed that it did its job of underlining
the drama as it unfolded.

EXAMPLE 2

sha - dows now are long - er,   for the sha - dows now are long - er.

The writing of a pop song caused some difficulty. I was given this lyric and asked to set it:

> Shut that gate, leave your troubles behind you,
> And go to a place where those others won't find you.
> Lose yourself in the noise and the hurry,
>   If you like, girl, I'll see you there.
>
> Feel the pulse of the fast-moving city
> As you walk down the road where the lights are so pretty;
> Feel the wind in your hair as you step on the highway.
>   If you like . . . (*etc.*)
>
> 'Cos I know the place
> Where the music is fine and the lights are always low,
> I know a place where we can go.
>
> You're gonna like it there I know,
> And I know the place where we can go.
> This is the place for us, I know,
> Yes, I know the place where we can go.

My difficulty in writing a pop tune to these words was not caused by the words themselves; I thought they were good. It was caused by the fact that I am not a teenager, and have therefore abandoned the armoury of untutored enthusiasm and arbitrary likes and dislikes which sway the decisions of both fans and fashioners of genuine pop music. I did eventually contrive a setting (see Example 3, 'I know the place'). We taught the tune phrase by phrase to a local group, 'All Things Sweet', who then worked out an authentic backing which drove its penetrating tones into every corner of the auditorium. Amplification – a force not to be trifled with – carried the

EXAMPLE 3

1. Shut that gate, leave your trou - bles be - hind __ you, and
2. Feel the pulse of the fast mo - ving city, __ as you

go to a place where those oth - ers won't find you. Lose your -
walk down the road, where the lights are so pret - ty. Feel the

self in the noise and the hur - ry, If you like, girl _____ I'll
wind as you step on the high - way,

see you there. 'Cos I know the

place where the mu - sic is fine and the lights are al - ways low,

I know a place where we can go You're gon - na like it

there I know. I know the place where we can go

You're gon - na like it hon - ey, yes I know this is the place where

we can go. I know the place where we can go!

sensitive ballad singer high on the crest of the volume of sound and achieved
more or less what we needed.

The same could in fact be said for the musical side of the production as a
whole. This was due in no small degree to the identity of aims achieved by
musicians, scriptwriters and producer. One of the most rewarding aspects of
the production for me was the close rapport we built up as a team intent on
a common goal.

11

Theatre in education

ROSEMARY BIRBECK and JUDITH and STUART BENNETT

There are a growing number of Theatre in Education teams attached to professional repertory theatres in Great Britain. Such enterprises have invariably come about through the practical influence of leaders in the community who are concerned with the overall education of their children. It is this awareness of some city councils and education authorities which makes it possible for children – and, in turn, adults – to become conscious of the importance of drama with its variety of forms and its role of fulfilling basic needs in society. The writers portray practical aspects of their work among the children of Coventry, their headquarters being the Belgrade Theatre in the heart of the city. Music – implying both the use of functional sounds and special effects, as well as the ballad – is a vital and necessary ingredient in the day-to-day work of the actor–teacher. It is illuminating to observe that such music is encouraged in performances, where it reinforces or makes clear a dramatic situation, as shown by the local documentary which I had the good fortune to take part in during a conference for teachers and children in Coventry.

Rosemary Birbeck described how the venture came into being and, with the help of two members of the team, Judith and Stuart Bennett, outlines the kind of work that has been developed.

Rosemary Birbeck taught drama at Hammersmith County School, then at Isleworth Polytechnic. She was head of Theatre in Education at the Belgrade Theatre from 1966 to 1970.

Judith Bennett wrote scripts for educational television before joining Theatre in Education in 1967.

Stuart Bennett read English at Cambridge, worked for the BBC, and taught in Leeds and Salford before joining Theatre in Education in 1967. He became head of Theatre in Education in 1970.

THEATRE IN EDUCATION

The Belgrade Theatre was opened in 1958 and, to Coventry's credit, was the first civic theatre to be built in the United Kingdom. From the start it was hoped that the theatre would be a vital force in the community, and a council directive to the Belgrade Theatre Trust urged that the theatre should examine ways in which it could assist the local education committee.

The theatre management felt strongly that it was the right of every child to have an experience of theatre. But what kind of 'theatre experience'? The traditional children's play takes place in a darkened auditorium on a proscenium stage. Was this the best line of development to take advantage of modern trends in education? Many teachers are concerned to stimulate the creativity of their children and to encourage their confidence to express ideas. Peter Slade in *Child Drama* had shown the value of children's drama and described the forms of expression basic to it. Brian Way, in *Development Through Drama*, had already devised a children's theatre with open staging, permitting a closer relationship between actor and audience, and with planned participation, drawing on the child's need to involve himself with character and situation. Could a repertory theatre forge links between drama and education? Through dramatic play the young child comes to terms with the imaginary and real world about him. The impact of good theatre extends the experience and enjoyment of life. Both are educative processes.

In 1964 the Belgrade Theatre, working in association with the Coventry Education Committee, produced the idea of Theatre in Education. The Belgrade Theatre would employ a specialist group of people as part of the company, able to work with teachers in the city's schools. These people could be primarily teachers or actors, but it was essential that all should have a sensitive awareness of the varied needs of children of different ages and abilities, a desire to experiment with drama as a teaching method and an ability to give children an experience of theatre relevant to their own needs and experiences. Hence the term actor–teacher.

The education committee appointed a panel of head teachers who met members of the theatre staff and discussed the aims and organization of this scheme, which was to provide an 'inspirational teaching service' for Coventry schools. The city council backed the idea by making available the sum of £15,000 for a pilot scheme. The full scheme began with an annual grant of £12,000. This has since been increased to £14,500. The Arts Council also supports the venture. The allocation of funds for the scheme has been subjected to the pressure of local government expenditure and economies. These jeopardized the future of the scheme in 1969–70, but money was eventually found to maintain the service and the present council has stated its intention to safeguard the scheme as a continuing feature of the city's educational programme.

Three-quarters of the total income goes towards paying the salaries of the members of the department. The other quarter provides money for the production expenses and running costs of the scheme. The department consists of nine actor-teachers, a designer and a secretary. The actor–teachers have varied backgrounds in the educational and professional theatre worlds and work as teaching teams in groups of four or as each programme demands. As head of department, I decide with which age-range of children and in which particular schools the groups will work. Discussions follow as to what the particular aim of each programme will be, and this will largely determine the content and methods of presentation. One general aim is common to all our work. Our intention is to give the individual child the opportunity to express and develop his own ideas and to form his own judgments; we ask him to respond physically, emotionally and intellectually in an imaginative situation. We provide the framework with which this can happen and as we are not obliged to operate with large audiences of children in order to cover our expenses, we can choose the size of the group according to the needs of each age-range. In the primary school this can be one class of thirty to forty children. We work in the school hall, but not on the stage. The story or adventure ranges freely round the floor of the hall and all the children are participating all the time. This is illustrated by *Danger Ahead*, a programme for remedial groups in the junior school, here described by Judith Bennett.

'DANGER AHEAD'

A class of less able ten- or eleven-year-olds are sitting in their classroom. The Storyteller, Roger Chapman, places a portable tape-recorder and a metronome on the desk, and sets the metronome ticking.

'What does this make you think of?'

'Ticking', says one child. 'A tap dripping', says another. A boy near the front of the class suggests a windscreen wiper, but then someone suggests a time-bomb. Roger agrees.

'This noise has been heard all over the world by radio, followed by this message.'

He switches on the tape-recorder.

'I am Professor Z. I have planted bombs in all the major cities of the world. The bombs will explode in three days' time if a million pounds in gold is not paid into my bank account at Zurich. You have been warned. The bombs are ticking.'

The children's attention has now been arrested. They recognize the beginning of a thriller and have been introduced to evil in the form of Professor Z. Roger continues the story.

'A few days ago a man was washed up on the beach. When he recovered his strength he travelled to London and demanded to see the prime minister. This man, Tom Blake, told the prime minister that he was a scientist who had been captured by Professor Z and made to work in his underground laboratory. He asked the prime minister for help to go with him to the island to destroy the laboratory. The prime minister offered him the army or the navy. But Tom said ...'

Suddenly the door opens and Gordon Wiseman enters as Tom Blake and says: 'I don't want the army or the navy, I want a small group of specially trained people.'

He looks at the class and senses the children's desire to join in.

'You can help me.'

The children respond.

'Right, there are some things you must know. The journey will be difficult and dangerous, but I have this to help us.'

He unfolds a clear, colourful map of an island surrounded by sea.

'The professor has his laboratory somewhere in these mountains. But we have to travel through the jungle, the swamp and these caves to reach it. There will be many hazards to overcome, but two people have offered to help us.'

Tom goes to the door and opens it. He introduces two new people to the class.

'This is Cora Williams who is an expert on mountaineering and cave exploration, and this is Judith Bennett who has experience of travelling through jungles and swamps. They can help us when we get to the island. I shall be in charge of the ship which will take us there. Now I shall divide you into three groups.'

He reads their names from a list supplied by the class teacher.

'Will these people go with Cora to learn about caves and mountains, and will these people go with Judith and learn about jungles and swamps. The other people stay here with me.'

In ten minutes we have gripped the attention of the children. We have given them a job to learn and by referring to them by name and asking for their help we have given them a responsibility within the context of the story. The class is now divided into three groups. My group accompany me to one end of the hall and we sit on the floor. I learn their Christian names as quickly as possible, and ask them what they know about jungles.

'There are lots of trees ... and wild animals. It's dark.'

'Is it dangerous?'

'Yes, there are snakes that can make themselves look like branches of a tree.'

'How about a swamp, what do you think that's like?'

'A swamp can suck you in. It's like quicksand ...'

'It's steamy. Sometimes it bubbles .. alligators live in swamps, and crocodiles.'

I show them jungle photographs and swamp pictures. We discuss them.

Every child has now some idea of a jungle and swamp.

'How should we travel through a jungle?'

'We'd have to be quiet.'

'Tell us why.'

'Because of the wild animals, and there might be natives who'd attack us.'

I comment on the need to move as silently as possible, and I make a mental note of other suggestions. We start building the jungle and swamp, using any gymnasium apparatus that seems suitable, including dinner chairs and tables in the corner. I then go to where a buck (gym horse) stands in the corner.

'Will you help me to pull this tree trunk over here?'

It is on castors, and we pull it into the jungle area.

'This tree trunk has fallen across the path, we'll have to climb over it. Wait a minute, look there! There's a nest of poisonous red ants under the log, so we'll have to climb over it trying not to disturb the ants. I'll lead the way.'

I climb carefully over the buck, the children follow.

I had checked with the class teacher before the children came into the hall that the buck was easily surmountable by even the most timid child. The obstacles that we would encounter in the jungle and swamp could get more hazardous; but that first fallen tree had to be simple so that each child's confidence in himself (as a jungle expert) was established. Suggestions about what we would find flowed from the children very quickly.

'There's a tunnel through the undergrowth – we could use those tables to make it.'

And so the tunnel is built and we practise crawling through it.

'We'll have to cross that river by swinging across on this creeper', another would suggest, pulling out a rope. A Tarzan shriek would burst forth, but I could control the yell by reminding the child that if we made a noise it would warn Professor Z of our approach.

Having acted upon their suggestions for the construction of the jungle, I organized the group to make a clearing in the jungle where we could light a fire, should we have to spend the night there. We collected wood. My reason for establishing a clearing was to provide a suitable place for the children to relax on the journey. The swamp was then built, possibly using mats or hoops for stepping-stones and marking a nest of alligators with chalk. When the two sections were built we met at the clearing in the jungle for a briefing session.

'We are the jungle and swamp experts. We will have to take the people from the other two groups safely through. It is our responsibility. We shall each take two people with us, one from Tom's group and one from

Cora's group and we shall lead them and tell them what to do. Now we will have one practice trip over our whole section to make sure we remember what to do.'

While my group were building the jungle and swamp at one end of the hall, Cora's group were building the caves at the other end, and Tom's group were planning the ship in the classroom. These simultaneous 'building' activities lasted twenty minutes. Then the children went for a break. If any children among my group were particularly boisterous I would try to give them something constructive to do. They were either scouts leading the way or guards on watch for danger when we encamped for the night. The children's imagination had been constantly aroused and stimulated, and they had been put into a situation where speech was often necessary, they had worked as a group and had been called upon to display some degree of physical courage.

Cora and I arranged to meet our groups in the classroom after break. Tom's group met in the hall to build the ship. They used balance benches and a unit of light-weight scaffolding giving a 7-foot high platform which we had brought with us. A messenger came to the classroom and told us that the crew were ready on board ship. We picked up the things we wanted to take with us, a rifle, a sharp knife, extra blankets and clothes and first-aid box, and we marched to the ship. Tom's crew piped us on board and showed us to our cabins. The sea journey began. All the props, of course, are imaginary.

The sound tape was our control factor and it governed the main incident on the sea voyage, a great storm. This was heralded by rough sea noises and the sound of the wind blowing up. Hatches were battened down and all sails lowered. Loose objects were made fast and we, the passengers, were sent below deck for safety. Our ship took a great buffeting in the storm but we finally made land safely. The crew dismantled the ship so that the professor could see no trace of our arrival. We then checked our position on the map that Tom had brought with him. We were all briefed by my jungle and swamp experts.

'The first thing you will find in the jungle is a fallen tree. It lies across the path, and you must climb over it, but under the tree is a nest of poisonous red ants. Don't disturb them or they may attack us.'

My group explain the jungle and take charge of people from other groups for the journey. The accompanying tape is full of strange tropical noises, weird bird-calls and animal shrieks. Suddenly we hear drum-beats. Everyone drops to the ground and is as still as possible. The drum-beats fade away.

'What was that Judith ?'

'I don't know. What do you think?'

'It was the professor's spies', someone suggests. 'He's got the natives on his side.'

'We'll have to be extra careful', says Tom. 'Time is running out.'

We work our way through the jungle to the clearing where we decide to rest for the night. The guards are positioned, the fire is lit. Supper is cooked and eaten, and we quietly sing a song around the camp fire before going to sleep. We are awoken the next morning by the birds and animals. We must re-assemble in single file to get through the swamp. When we have completed the journey through the swamp, my group hand over the responsibility to Cora's group. Along with Tom's group we must learn about the mountains and caves from the experts. Suddenly, when we are deep in the caves we hear the voice of Professor Z.

'I have blocked the entrance to the cave with a fall of rock.'

We hear a great rumble of rocks falling.

'You shall not escape, I shall blow up the cave you are in.'

'We must find a way out', says Cora. 'Can anyone see a rock or boulder that we can push aside?'

A few children start to get frightened.

'There's a way out here', says Tom.

He pushes aside a rostrum block and we are now in the passage leading to the laboratory. The ticking gets louder. We discover the scaffolding, which now in our imagination becomes a machine full of levers, knobs and dials. We pull, push and wind, and to our relief the machine stops ticking. Our sense of relief is enormous, but one child notices a strange figure approaching. Tom shouts: 'It's Professor Z. Stand back!'

'You think you've won, but you've not escaped yet. You must fight me for your life.'

A fierce sword fight takes place. The children cheer Tom, and he finally triumphs. The professor collapses.

'We must escape immediately, the island will blow up if the machine is stopped before the bombs explode.'

We run to the shore and row away from the island. There is a loud explosion as the island blows up. We row out of the hall and into the class-room, where the tension relaxes. We sit on the floor. The journey has taken about three-quarters of an hour and we are physically tired. Tom tells us that Professor Z will no longer trouble the world and he thanks us all for our help. The children feel a strong sense of achievement and are pleased with themselves and each other. We have a final talk to our groups and say our goodbyes; we get the children to relax their bodies and their minds and we leave the classroom.

After each session we talk to the class teachers and ask them for comments. Generally they find it useful to observe their children, and they are often surprised at the degree of concentration and involvement shown by their class. Teachers also comment that children who are normally scared of climbing on P.E. equipment show no fear when the equipment is put in an imaginative situation and becomes, for example, a tree. Many teachers, stimulated by our example, plan to continue using our ideas and develop play into constructive drama in their own classes.

The programme described above concentrated on physical involvement, but the underlying experience was facing danger. A great deal of writing, tape-recording and painting was stimulated by it. Programmes which have used the power of myth or legend as a basis have had similar success. In a recent infant programme, *How Rain came to Hweng Chow*, a class of infant children became the rice-growing villagers of Hweng Chow and had to accomplish many tasks set by the Dragon Gods before the Dragon King would bring the much-needed rain. *How the Animals Helped Ram and Sita* is an infant programme based on an Indian legend. The children listen to the story told by an actor–teacher in the classroom and act it out, using models of the main characters which they have made themselves. Then, in the hall, the children become the animals in the story and help the actor–teacher playing Ram to rescue the Princess Sita from the terrible ten-headed monster, Ravana. Both these parts are played by actor–teachers in costume, using masks and headdresses.

Recent excavations of a Roman fort on the outskirts of the city inspired a team-teaching project which brought one class of top juniors as Roman soldiers into conflict with another class of juniors as the Celtic farmers already established in the area. We organized a sequence of events: the Roman occupation of the area; building the fort; taxing the natives; suppressing a revolt. Archaeological evidence suggests that this may all have happened in A.D. 60, at the time of the Boudicca rebellion, although the problems of conflicting cultures and human relationships which ensued have a much wider application. The class teachers came to two practical working sessions after school in which we explored preparatory and follow-up work.

Social, moral and political problems are often the starting-point for secondary programmes which are sometimes devised in conjunction with a particular play running at the Belgrade Theatre. A Theatre in Education project for school-leavers in the summer term set up an imaginary community, 'Stoke Hill Wood'. Through group improvisations, pupils became identified with members of families living in different types of property in the area, old or new, council or private. After the initial family scenes, they polarized into age groups at the youth club, the football club, the social club and the good companions club, only to learn that they were about to lose their premises as the result of a council redevelopment plan. A councillor, played by an actor–teacher, outlines the plan at a public meeting where the pupils had the opportunity as the characters they had established to voice their support or disapproval of the plan, and to assess the priorities of the community. This experience was extended further when the same pupils attended a performance of John Arden's *Live Like Pigs* at the Belgrade Theatre, and saw problems of misunderstanding and intolerance in a community pushed to extremes.

Secondary school programmes usually combine classroom teaching sessions with performances in the school hall. In the performance we work as actors portraying characters and speaking dialogue which we may have scripted or which we are improvising with the pupils. If the pupils are participating physically in the action all the time, we move freely around the hall and then only work with a maximum of two classes. If the pupils are to be an audience most of the time, we act in the 'round' with the pupils on four sides. They are, however, an informed audience. Preparatory work will have given them an experience of the ideas to be presented, or it may have given them a group identity in the context of the story, with a particular point of view they will be encouraged to express.

This preparatory work is most important. We work in the classroom in pairs. This eases the burden of researching the relevant information. It also gives the class the added stimulus of listening to another voice as we build up the necessary background. In this 'team teaching' we use question and answer, and visual aids supplied by our designer. We set up situations for speech improvisation in pairs and groups which will enable us to examine the arguments and characterizations that emerge. We try to influence teachers to use these methods, and we involve them actively in both preparation and follow-up work. Our programme has little significance if it is an isolated event in the school curriculum. We wish it to be part of the teacher's own project. Teachers are asked to attend courses and workshop sessions before and during the run of the programme. The sessions are practical and give them an opportunity of working at drama at their own level, and we are able to exchange ideas on the treatment of the material in our programme. We discuss in what ways the teachers can help in introducing some of the material before we come and how they will follow up the stimulus we give with further work in drama, creative writing, music, art, craft and general research into the topic.

The Coventry Weavers is such a project which was toured a second time at the schools' request. It is here described by Stuart Bennett.

'THE COVENTRY WEAVERS'

During the school holidays, Colin White helped me to investigate the history of Coventry in the nineteenth century. The subject attracted us – why should this small town, weaving silk ribbon, have been the one that pioneered the modern motor car? Frances Colyer and Judith Bennett joined us, and we began to wonder what life was like for the ordinary people of the city in the nineteenth century.

Our research was carried out in the Coventry and Warwickshire local history library. There we read newspapers, government reports and broadsheets. We found the autobiography of a self-educated weaver, Joseph Gutteridge, now reprinted in *Master and Artisan in Victorian England* (Evelyn, Adams and Mackay, 1969). We also consulted *The Industrial Revolution in Coventry* by John Prest (Oxford, 1960).

The story of the town, we discovered, centred on a community of cottage weavers striving to maintain their independence, and adapting to the factory age, only to suffer a disastrous slump in 1860. There was widespread unemployment and the population actually declined. Silk was finished, the town needed a new trade. James Starley provided this with the bicycle, and from that development came the motor car industry.

This basic material suggested two lines of development. First, improvised drama sessions exploring the lives of the weavers; the social effects of the coming of the machine and the factory. Second, a regional documentary as pioneered by Peter Cheeseman and his company at the Victoria Theatre, Stoke-on-Trent; using dramatized scenes, movement, colour and music to recreate the story of the town. No heroes had emerged in this story, but Joseph Gutteridge's life-story provided an ideal narrative link.

We decided to visit each school for a day. In the morning we would explore the background and lives of the weavers, using the methods of classroom drama. Our aim was to develop an identification with the weavers and the fate of the town. In the afternoon we would perform a theatrical documentary, integrating the pupils' morning work into the action at key points.

CLASSROOM SESSION

I am facing a class of fourth- or fifth-year pupils who have done no drama. How can I begin to communicate the enthusiasm which the team feels towards the project to them? I hold up a photograph of surviving weavers' cottages.

'Have any of you seen buildings like these?'

Most have seen them on the way to the football ground. Someone may have heard of silk-ribbon weaving. I show them a piece of broad silk ribbon and a picture of a dress for which it would be made. We discuss the difficulties of a trade depending upon fashion.

'What was life like then?'

I have two pieces of evidence, both notices; I hold up one headed 'Riotous Assemblies of Weavers'. It is a warning from the magistrates that they will take severe action if the weavers continue to traverse the streets in a manner inciting terror and alarm in the peaceable inhabitants. The date is 1835. The second offers a reward of £50 for the apprehension of the weavers who destroyed a master's house. The date, 1800.

'What could lie behind these two incidents?'

A discussion follows. Men riot if they cannot afford food for their families, or if their work is threatened.

'What would happen nowadays?'

We – the class and myself – establish that we are dealing with life before the welfare state and workers' rights. By this stage there should be a feeling of partnership in common research. Moreover, the topic we are considering must appear to them to be worthy of their attention. The weavers have been introduced. We know something about them. Drama can begin to help us to extend our understanding of them, but it cannot be divorced from the relationship between teacher and class.

'I would now like to explore some of the problems the weavers would meet. I'm going to ask you to help me by being the weavers.'

No discussion here. Having begun to introduce involvement, a decisive manner helps, as any apprehension by the teacher will be felt by the class. I have been using question and answer for some time. They need a 'warm-up' activity to free voices and limbs.

'As weavers you will need to know how to weave.'

I explain warp, weft, shuttle and reed with a model loom.

'The pedals select the pattern; the shuttle is thrown from hand to hand carrying the weft; the reed beats the weft into place. Hold out your right hand. That hand is holding the shuttle. Press the pedals; one, two! Throw the shuttle across! beat up with the reed!'

We practise the rhythmic mime: one, two, shuttle, reed. It is a concentration exercise as you must remember which hand the shuttle is in. Some of the class manage well, but it produces laughter when they make a mistake. Others do not yet join in whole-heartedly. A colleague, Frances Colyer, takes over.

'We asked you to follow the motion of weaving for half a minute. What kind of skill does it demand? How many hours a day would a weaver do that for?'

She begins to build up a picture of the cottage-weaver's life from the simple mime. The weavers are independent. They work when they want to, on their own looms, in their own cottages. She recites a rhyme:

'"Weavers: drunk on Sunday; headache on Monday; work on Tuesday; eight hours Wednesday; ten hours Thursday; all day Friday; paid on Saturday – drunk on Sunday ..." Work with the person next to you in your desks. The person on the left of each pair, you're a weaver. The other person is the father or wife. Weaver, you began work at six this morning. It's now eight and you're thinking of stopping for something to eat. Father or wife, it's Friday, rent day and you've no money, tell him of your difficulties. Weavers throw the shuttle and ask for something to eat. Begin the conversation – now!'

Each pair begins to talk. A certain amount of reluctance is apparent, but some pairs have obviously caught the idea. After general activity is established, questions follow.

'Let's overhear some Friday conversations in the cottages.'

She asks a pair she knows has something to offer.

'Where's my breakfast?'

'You don't get anything to eat till you finish that ribbon.'

'Why not?'

'You booze all weekend, and then I'm short at the end of the week.'

Another pair is asked and they also pick up the idea of the weaver drinking at the weekend.

'How am I going to feed my eight children?'

This makes us laugh, but Frances asks whether this would not be quite possible at that time. For the third pair she asks one of the reluctant ones who now have enough to build on from what they've heard. The weavers are beginning to assume character.

I take over and explain that the weavers are on piece work. Each type and pattern has a price, and these are printed. I hold up the list of prices for 1816.

'What will happen if any weaver undercuts this list?'

We discover that if any one man works for less than the list it's an opportunity for the master to pay everyone less. No honourable weaver will take less than the list price. I set up a conversation in pairs. The weaver has completed his ribbon on Saturday, but the master offers him 12s., not the 14s. to which he is entitled. The weaver tells his father or wife, and they discuss whether to take the 12s. Again I allow the general activity to start. Last time some pupils did not respond. This time they understand what's being asked of them and they realize they can contribute. We listen again to short conversations.

'You'll have to take 12s., it's better than nothing.' 'No, we must make a stand on this.'

They are now ready to join up in pairs.

'You've talked it over in your own family, but what about the other weavers? Turn to the weavers in the next cottage. Discuss with them what you think the weavers would do in a case like this. Begin now!'

While the general conversation starts, I talk to four weavers:

'I've been into Broadgate and I've heard why we're not getting the usual price. One of the masters has installed steam machines. They can do the work of four weavers, and women can work them. You'll be out of a job. Go and tell everyone!'

When this news has been passed among the class during the general discussion, I stand on a chair.

'Weavers! I've called you to this meeting on Greyfriars' Green, where we discuss our affairs, because we've all heard about Mr Josiah Beck and how he'll be putting us out of a job with his steam machines. What are we going to do?'

'Burn his house!' 'Kill him!' 'Throw bricks through his windows.' 'Destroy his machines!'

'Do you think that will help us?'

'Yes. If his machines are destroyed he'll have to employ us on the old terms.'

'The last time we had a dispute we organized a petition. Shall we organize one now?'

The fury has abated a little. In character we settle down to a discussion of the best tactics. A petition will keep us on the right side of the law. Some feel it will take too long. We need a show of force. 'Burn down his workshop.' 'If you're caught you'll be hanged.' 'I'll take the risk; better than starving.'

Eventually we take a vote and agree to go down to Beck's factory and demand to have our position explained. If we don't like what we hear we've no choice but to resort to violence. I close the meeting and the group sits down.

'On 7 November 1831 the weavers must have had a meeting very like that one. Some went to petition the Mayor. While they were there they saw a column of smoke. Beck's factory had been fired.'

SPEECH IMPROVISATION AND MOVEMENT

Beginning drama with adolescents with a movement session has certain risks if they are not used to it. Building speech improvisation has the advantage that it can begin in the classroom which is familiar to the pupils. All you ask them to do is to talk to their partners about a specific topic. If they are all working simultaneously they will not be inhibited from starting. One rule: no one may disturb or distract a pair who are demonstrating their conversation. When a pair break into laughter themselves it is better to take them quietly back to the start than to abandon it. Keep the scenes short. Stop them before invention flags. The major difficulty is not in starting this method but in developing the serious thought behind each scene, without which it is of little value. Listening to a scene is as important as demonstrating it, and discussion can arise about whether the people in the scene were truthfully portrayed. Work in pairs can be built into work in fours and so into crowd reaction; by dwelling upon the realities of the situation the crowd can emerge as a group of conflicting individuals rather than an undifferentiated football crowd. At the end of the crowd discussion the group were standing and beginning to use their bodies, shaking fists, gesturing and finding desks in the way.

We are now going to carry out an investigation into the burning down of the factory. Frances takes over.

'We will follow the events of the day, and so we will need space.'

The desks are cleared and she takes them through a simple movement sequence.

'This picture shows a steam engine. Notice the pressure gauge, the pipes, the valves and the boiler. You all have a steam engine in front of you. Walk around it. It is strange; you have never seen one before. Touch it. Take a screwdriver and take the pressure gauge to bits carefully. Throw them away. Pull one of the pipes.'

Frances uses a tambour (small hand drum). With each blow they wrench off a part of their steam engine until they have destroyed it. Each movement is to one beat. Now they are ready to work in pairs.

'Find a partner. One of you is going to punch the other. But one rule: there must be no actual touching. You are weavers; you are angry; you are trying to knock your opponent down. Feel your knuckles. Decide where you are going to strike. Opponent respond by flinching wherever a blow is aimed.'

They build up a sequence of six blows, as in a stage fight, using the drum as a signal for each blow. In this way the violence is slowed down, and we can see the effectiveness of a pair whose sequence is varied and realistic.

GROUP SCENES

We now divide. Half the group devises what one group of weavers would have done. My group are to examine how the power looms were destroyed. Four become mechanics. We discuss their attitude to the weavers.

'We're skilled men, not like the old-fashioned weavers.'

They go off and set up a workshop, using desks. I then discuss the weavers' attitude with the others.

'Some would be frightened.' 'I'd break the machinery.' 'We might be for talking first, then using violence.'

I start the sequence. The weavers come to a meeting and the hotheads persuade the others to go to the factory. As they approach the mechanics there is a general milling about, and the mechanics bunch up at the door. I stop them for discussion. Did the more timid people have a chance to say anything at the meeting? What's going to happen now? I know that if I let it go on without a discussion it will degenerate into a scrimmage. Do the mechanics know the weavers are coming? How do the weavers get through the door? What will their reaction to the machines be? Remember they have never seen any before.

The scene resumes. The weavers beat on the door. One mechanic shouts to know what they want. They can't come in. The weavers put their shoulders to the door; the mechanics relent. They can come in and look. Slowly they file in and finger the machinery. The mechanics explain what it is, but are suspicious. I stop the scene.

'What starts off a riot?'

'An argument.'

'People pushing.'

'What would you do if someone pushes you?'

'Push back!'

'What would start this riot?'

'A weaver could touch something and break it.'

'The mechanic might insult him.'

The scene is now in its last section. I tell them I'll give six claps of the hand to control the fight, then I appoint one weaver who will see the cavalry riding down Broadgate. They resume. The mechanics explain the machines. One says it will do the work of four weavers. A weaver objects and pushes him on to the looms. The fight starts. The looms are destroyed. The cavalry are seen, and the weavers flee. Discussion. What went wrong? We agree that the fight was lacking in detail and that there should be more speech. Also when one conversation in going on the others should listen. We are now ready to run the sequence through. The drum is the signal for activity to stop and gives the speed of the fight. The real control lies in the extent to which one has established the basic seriousness and reality of the situation, and in the degree to which each pupil feels he is contributing. If he feels responsible for a part he will not want to sabotage it.

Frances has finished her section, and we put the riot together. First her group run their sequence then we run ours. The whole sequence concerns violence, but we have not dealt with it simply because it is exciting. The riot crystallizes the attitudes of the weavers at a particular moment. At the end of the sequence three men are arrested. These are the pupils who have developed the most militant characters. We give them the names of the men who were arrested in 1831, Burbury, Sparkes, Toogood. What is our attitude to them as weavers? To some they are heroes who stood up for us. To others they are rash men who should have waited for the result of the petition.

The topic has been concerned with people, and what we have explored together is basically a moral decision. The drama has evolved from the problem these people were faced with, and has helped us gain some personal insight into the issues. The issues themselves must be real if the drama is to be real, otherwise it is just a superficial injection of excitement into a dead topic.

The session with class A just described, lasted until break. At the same time Judith and Colin worked with class B and improvised another part of the same riot, an assault on the master Josiah Beck. Further arrests were made.

After break we worked with classes C and D and dealt with the later period, when street riots were no longer effective and organized strike action grew up.

THE PERFORMANCE

The four classes come together for the performance in the afternoon. They sit on four sides of a square, the action takes place in the middle. There is no stage lighting, as many school halls do not black out.

We need to arrest the audience's attention and set the style – a story told for you, the weavers. We begin with the song 'The Jolly Weaver'* and mime a weaving operation (see Example 1).

EXAMPLE 1

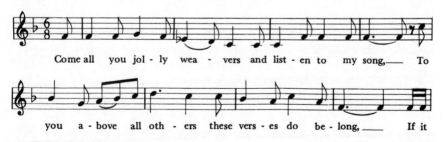

Come all you jol - ly wea - vers and list - en to my song,— To
you a - bove all oth - ers these vers - es do be - long, — If it

---

* We are grateful to Roy Palmer for permission to reproduce this version of 'The Jolly Weaver'.

12

were not for the wea - ver our backs might all go bare,___ And

CHORUS

so go all___ to-geth - er, as our fore-fa - thers were. And

so go all to - geth - er as our fore-fa - thers were.___

Young Joe is seen at charity school where he narrowly escapes a thrashing: then at home with a tyrannical stepmother. At the age of thirteen he is apprenticed as a weaver, and while an apprentice joins the band of angry men who go down to Beck's factory to seek justice.

COURT USHER: Coventry Lent Assizes 1832. Everyone rise for his Lordship.

The whole audience stand. The judge enters. When they sit it is natural for them to talk. They are now in the public gallery of the courtroom. Everyone knows something of the riot, but no one knows all the details. The pupils arrested in the morning's improvisations are sitting together. They stand.

JUDGE: Burbury, Sparkes, Toogood, Day, Deeming, Westwick, Barton. You are charged with unlawfully rioting and destroying the house of Josiah Beck in this city with the machinery and steam engine therein.

Some of the public gallery may start to applaud.

JUDGE: I must remind all concerned of the gravity of this offence. The law states that all riotous assemblies must be restrained. The penalty for this offence is death.

The audience have a motivation to respond emotionally to the evidence we are about to hear. The more involved they were in the classroom sessions, the more specific and sincere their response will be now. The judge is strict but fair, and controls any extreme disorder.

An actor, the prosecution lawyer, questions a boy (or girl) as Josiah Beck. The pupil doesn't know what he is going to be asked; he replies from his recollection of the improvisation. What happened on the day in question? He was assaulted or 'donkeyed'. By whom? He identifies some of the accused. What kind of employer is he? The trade is backward. He wants to improve it for the good of everyone. The mechanics are questioned. The weavers who destroyed the power looms are identified. The mechanics share Beck's attitude to progress. The public gallery does not. If he senses any awkwardness among his witnesses, the prosecution lawyer asks for details to deepen their concentration, but his principal control is his own involvement in the issues.

When, as defence lawyer, I ask the accused to speak in their own defence the weavers are ready to put their case to the court. Again the pupils do not know what questions I shall ask. They speak from their own understanding of these men. Why was Mr Beck 'donkeyed'? They wanted to make an example of him. Why? Other masters would start underpaying.

They use the background material they explored in the morning. But what they say now may save them from the gallows. We can't live on 12s. a week – I've children to support – So have I – I can't afford to hire my loom if my weekly payment is low. Why was the machinery destroyed? We are afraid it will put us cottage weavers out of work.

DEFENCE LAWYER: Your Lordship these men are not rogues and vagabonds. They are respectable hard-working men who went to Mr Beck's new factory to ask for a fair deal.

The courtroom waits. No one knows the outcome of the trial. The actors are in costume, the pupils, boys or girls, are not. Theatrical convention is not relevant here. Together we have created a moment when the fate of these men hangs in the balance. The judge speaks slowly and deliberately. Four men will be charged with assault but are acquitted of factory-wrecking. The others, Burbury, Sparkes and Toogood are found guilty. They stand. The judge dons the black cap and pronounces the death sentence. The court rises.

Historically, the defence mitigation plea was accepted, the men were reprieved and transported. They were indeed ordinary hard-working men, and the trial needed no histrionics to make it gripping. Running through the whole sequence is the nearness to subsistence level at which the weavers lived.

We now pick up this fact and Joe's story in the documentary presentation. He meets a servant girl, marries for love and so escapes from the tyranny of his stepmother. He has set up home before he has saved enough to buy a loom, however, and is never to be independent.

At this point we wanted to establish the importance of fashion, and use a music hall sequence based on a Victorian drawing-room ballad on fashion. So now ornate chords on the piano herald the Triumphant Engagement of two Captivating young Ladies, who sing of the Glories of Fashion (see Example 2).

EXAMPLE 2

One singer is dressed in red, white and blue ribbons, the other's dress is decorated with the fleur-de-lys. A comic dispute breaks out in song about which ribbons are superior, the English or the French. This sequence was not mere light relief. If English ribbons were not in favour with the ladies, the Coventry weaver was out of work.

Joe tells us of the fear of the workhouse. Here we took a parliamentary report on the social conditions of the weavers, and dramatized it. Joe himself falls on hard times. Without a loom of his own he is among the first victims of any slump. With his young wife and family he is reduced to living in a slum court. He has no alternative but to go into the new factories. Times are changing, and a comic song of the period, 'I can't find my way in Coventry', reflects the singer's bewilderment at the town's industrial expansion (see Example 3).

EXAMPLE 3

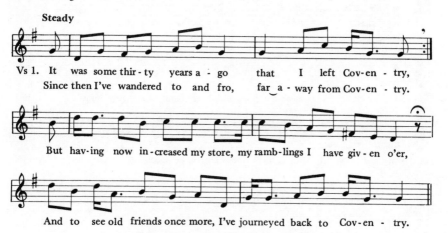

Vs 1. It was some thir-ty years a-go that I left Cov-en-try,
Since then I've wandered to and fro, far a-way from Cov-en-try.

But hav-ing now in-creased my store, my ramb-lings I have giv-en o'er,

And to see old friends once more, I've journeyed back to Cov-en-try.

Vs 2. A huge Gas Chimney built on tick,
To smoke-light poor old Coventry,
Stands like a fourth steeple built of brick,
And looks very queer in Coventry.
The Hill-Fields too, so green before,
With a New Town is Cover'd o'er,
'Till Foleshill very soon I'm sure,
Will be a part of Coventry.

The second half of the documentary followed an interval, and dealt with the Factory Age. We had been concerned to use music only where it amplified our theme. It should not be thought of as a means of enlivening an otherwise dull subject. Here we needed to change the mood. Roy Palmer of the Birmingham Folk Club had been advising us and he suggested a rallying song of the early unions (see Example 4).

EXAMPLE 4

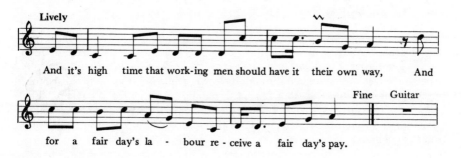

And it's high time that work-ing men should have it their own way, And

Fine   Guitar

for a fair day's la-bour re-ceive a fair day's pay.

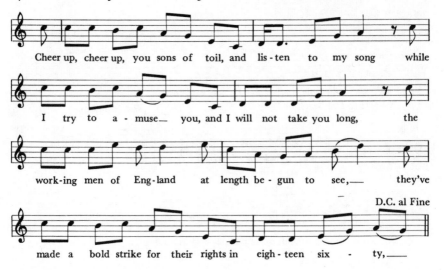

Cheer up, cheer up, you sons of toil, and lis-ten to my song while

I try to a-muse— you, and I will not take you long, the

work-ing men of Eng-land at length be-gun to see,— they've

D.C. al Fine

made a bold strike for their rights in eigh-teen six - ty,—

Joe is now a foreman. A dispute with the employers breaks out and a strike is called. This is the second involvement section. Classes C and D have improvised the background to the strike with blacklegs and pickets. They call out classes A and B and the whole audience come into the acting area. It is 1860. They meet and strike for workers' rights. Time passes, trade leaves the town. Will they go back? Their funds give out. Some relent. Each weaver makes his own decision. Four weeks pass. A trade union leader appeals to them to stand firm. Two months. A local clergyman attempts to arbitrate. His arguments are sound, but if they go back to work they've made a stand for nothing. Finally, starvation stares them in the face. The government signs a Free-Trade Treaty with France. Cheap French ribbons flood the market. Coventry is finished.

We return to the documentary. Joe and the weavers are destitute. A song written at the time – 'The Weaver'* – with the refrain 'He's only a weaver whom nobody owns' is sung unaccompanied (see Example 5). The audience listen with an inner identification with the people whose heartbreak and poverty is described.

---

* Joseph Gutteridge writing on the Coventry ribbon-weavers' strike of 1860 in his autobiography, *Lights and Shadows in the Life of an Artisan* (p. 153): 'A sheet of verses was circulated through the town, composed by Thomas Rushton, a compositor on the *Coventry Herald*, a parody on Tom Hood's poem "The Pauper". This song was sung by bodies of distressed weavers, who marched in procession through the streets, or when they proceeded to and from their work on the commons.'

EXAMPLE 5

Vs 1. Who is that man coming up the street with wear-ied man-ner and
      face that tells of__ care and grief and in hope seems to have

shuf-fling feet with a
lost be-lief. But take no heed of his sighs and groans, his

care-worn face and ag-on-y moans, for wick-ed-ness past he

D.C. Vs 2.

now a-tones, he's on-ly a wea-ver whom no-bod-y owns.

Vs. 2. His wife, I know, has a face as wan;
       They've a home 'tis true but the furniture's gone
       And when the children the father meet,
       They ask him with tears for something to eat.

With the arrival of James Starley, hope returns. He needs skilled men to make bicycles. The mood changes and we are in a music hall listening to ditties about the new-fangled bicycle, and the even more outrageous motor car. The new Coventry is here. Our story is complete except for one backward glance over his life by Joe.

Now may prosperity be the lot
Of poor old Coventry,
And all have enough to boil the pot,
Like the good old time in Coventry,
And may the Unions all increase,
Till not a Black Sheep shows his fleece,
And tyranny for ever cease,
To ruin poor old Coventry.

The programme described by Stuart Bennett uses the language of theatre, mime, movement, dialogue and song to make memorable a theme already explored by the audience. The theatre element evolves from the basic theme. It is not the exercise of an art for its own sake.

During the first four years of the scheme, Theatre in Education work has been presented in nearly all of Coventry's 169 schools, and the team has also worked with students at the local college of education and the technical colleges.

I make regular reports on our work and on future plans at meetings of the advisory committee of head teachers, representing all types of schools in the city. I ask guidance on what policy I shall adopt in selecting schools, and seek their help in order to ensure that our work is widely understood. Teachers must be present when we are working with the children if there is to be a follow-up. Schools are free to apply for a visit, or I telephone a head and suggest we come. We are usually enthusiastically received, and the impact we make on pupils is immediate, but owing to our infrequent visits, transitory. We hope that the impact on teachers is more lasting, but this seems to vary enormously. For some, we are merely a complication on the timetable. More optimistically, we hope we are providing a stimulus to teachers, especially those who may have lost interest or may feel that drama is a waste of time, producing no valuable results. Drama is usually considered suitable for the less able pupils, and of course claims can rightly be made for its therapeutic value. It is much harder to get teachers, particularly in secondary schools hidebound by the examination syllabus, to appreciate that the releasing of the imagination of pupils of all abilities through drama can lead to a fuller understanding and enjoyment of so many worth-while topics. When we have organized day courses attended by the teachers of the classes we are going to visit, a valid collaboration has resulted. Our aim is to suggest methods of working which will be valid for the whole year, not just the day of our visit. Very few Coventry schools have special provision for drama on the time-table. We are concerned that drama should not be thought to be solely the province of the drama specialist. We feel that a teacher who is sensitive to children's creative activity can channel it into improvised drama. It is not the actor or theatrically inclined person who is necessarily good at bringing children's work to fruition. The work we have devised allows children of all abilities to experience life through their imagination. It is an attempt to harness the skills and resources of theatre to the aims of creative teaching.

Further reading

Addison, Richard. *Make Music*, and *Children Make Music*. Edinburgh: Holmes McDougall Ltd, 1967.

Adland, D. E. *The Group Approach to Drama*. 4 vols. London: Longmans, 1967.

Alington, A. F. *Drama and Education*. Oxford: Basil Blackwell, 1961.

Barnfield, Gabriel. *Creative Drama in Schools*. London: Macmillan, 1968.

Bentley, Eric. *The Theory of the Modern Stage*. London: Penguin, 1968.

Billing, R. N. P. and Clegg, J. D. *Teaching Drama*. London: Univ. of London Press, 1965.

Bowra, C. M. *Primitive Song*. London: Weidenfeld and Nicolson, 1962.

Bryce, A. E. *The Rhythm of Sound*. Sydney: McGraw-Hill, 1969.

Chilver, Peter. *Staging a School Play*. London: Batsford Ltd, 1967.

Cook, H. Caldwell. *The Play Way*. London: Heinemann, 1917.

Courtney, Richard. *Drama for Youth*. London: Cassell, 1964.
   Play, Drama and Thought. Cassell, 1968.

Dwyer, Terence. *Opera in Your School*. London: O.U.P., 1964.

Gomme, Alice B. *Traditional Games*. N.Y.: Dover, 1964.
   Children's Singing Games. Dover, 1967.

Hodgson, J. and Richards, E. *Improvisation, Discovery and Creativity in Drama*. London: Methuen, 1968.
   Living Expression. Ginn, 1968. (2 books.)

Joubert, John and Holbrook, David. *The Quarry: An Opera for Young Players*. London: Novello, 1966.

Kerman, Joseph. *Opera as Drama*. N.Y.: Vintage Books, 1952.

Martin, William and Vallins, Gordon. *Exploration Drama*. London: Evans, 1968. (4 books.)

Massialas, B. G. and Zevin, J. *Creative Encounters in the Classroom*. N.Y./London: John Wiley and Sons, 1967.

Mellers, Wilfrid. *Caliban Reborn*. London: Gollancz, 1968.
   Life Cycle. Cambridge: C.U.P., 1969.

Muir, Willa. *Living with Ballads*. London: Hogarth Press, 1965.

Opie, I. and P. *The Lore and Language of School Children*. London: O.U.P., 1959.
   Children's Games in Street and Playgound. London: O.U.P., 1969.

Paynter, J. and Aston, P. *Sound and Silence*. Cambridge: C.U.P., 1970.

Sachs, Curt. *World History of the Dance*. N.Y.: Norton, 1963.

Self, George. *New Sounds in Class*. London: Universal Edition, 1967.

Siks, G. B. and Dunnington, H. B. *Children's Theatre and Creative Dramatics*. Seattle: Univ. of Washington, 1961.

Slade, Peter. *Child Drama*. London: Univ. of London Press, 1954.

Thackray, R. N. *Creative Music in Education*. London: Novello, 1965.

Way, Brian. *Development Through Drama*. London: Longmans, 1967.

Wiles, John and Garrard, Alan. *Leap to Life*. London: Chatto and Windus, 1965.

Willett, John. *The Theatre of Berthold Brecht*. London: Methuen, 1968.

Index

175